DATE DUE

FEB 21 1994	

BRODART   Cat. No. 23-221

Culture and Development

Culture and Development

Cultural Patterns in Areas of Uneven Development

K.C. Alexander

K.P. Kumaran

Sage Publications
New Delhi • Newbury Park • London

First published in 1992 by

Sage Publications India Pvt Ltd
32.M Block Market, Greater Kailash I
New Delhi 110 048

Sage Publications Inc
2455 Teller Road
Newbury Park, California 91320

Sage Publications Ltd
6 Bonhill Street
London EC2A 4PU

Published by Tejeshwar Singh for Sage Publications India Pvt Ltd, photo-typeset by Pagewell Photosetters, Pondicherry and printed at Chaman Enterprises, Delhi.

ISBN: 0–8039–9437–0 (U.S., Hb)
81–7036–293–8 (India, Hb)

Contents

List of Tables

Acknowledgements

We received help from various sources in the course of this study. While it is difficult to acknowledge such assistance individually, we would like to record our gratitude to T.L. Sankar, Director General, National Institute of Rural Development, Hyderabad, for his encouragement in the publication of this study. We are also grateful to S.R. Ramamurthy, former Director General of the Institute, for his support in the study.

For the collection of data, we were assisted by E.C. Jayakumar and K. Sumanchandra. Jayakumar assisted and supervised the fieldwork in Azamgarh, Saharanpur, and Trichur, and also supervised the coding of data and its preparation for analysis. Data analysis was conducted by J. Panduranga Rao and P. Satish Chandra. We are also grateful to S.V. Rangacharyulu, Asst Director (Statistics), for advising us on the statistical analysis of data. We would also like to thank V. Vijaya Lakshmi, Vara Prasad and D. Ramakrishna for typing the manuscript. However, we are solely responsible for any limitations in this work.

Hyderabad
March 1992

K.C. ALEXANDER
K.P. KUMARAN

1

Introduction

The objective of this study is to understand the pattern of culture in areas with varying levels of development. This has been done to understand the relevance of culture for social and economic development. As an introduction, the concept of culture and the processes through which it influences human action in general, and socio-economic action in particular, are briefly discussed.

and it shape our landscape.

Definition of Culture and its Characteristics

and

Definitions of the term 'culture' have changed from time to time. About a century ago, E.B. Tylor (1871) defined culture as 'that complex whole which includes knowledge, beliefs, art, morals, law, custom, and any other capabilities and habits acquired by man as a member of society'. Half a century later, A.L. Kroeber (1948) described culture as consisting of speech, knowledge, beliefs, customs, art, and technologies, ideals and rules; what is learned from other men, from elders, and what is added to it. This description of culture is very close to Tylor's earlier definition, implying that little progress was made in the concept of culture during this period. However, the definition of culture given by A.L. Kroeber and Clyde Kluckhohn in 1952 emphasised new dimensions of the concept. They stated that culture consists of patterns, explicit and implicit, of and for behaviour, acquired and transmitted by symbols, constituting the distinctive achievements of human groups, including their embodiment in artifacts; the essence of culture consists of traditional (i.e., historically derived and selected) ideas and especially their attached values; a culture system may, on the one hand, be considered as a product of action and, on the other, as a conditioning element of further action. In short, culture is the total social heritage acquired by man as a member of the society. This definition emphasises that culture is shared and has distinctive forms (patterns), that it shapes human behaviour, and its essence is the values embodied in the beliefs of the people. This makes value orientation patterns the essential feature of culture. Surrounding this core are other aspects of culture, such as empirical knowledge, technologies, religious beliefs, ideologies, skills and artifacts related to it.

Culture is often described as learned behaviour, to distinguish it from that aspect of behaviour caused by biological stimulation. As it is learned, it is transmitted from person to person, and from generation to generation. And, as it is cherished by a major section of the society, culture is said to be shared.

While anthropologists have been predominantly concerned with the patterning aspect of culture, it was sociologists, particularly Talcott Parsons (1951), who analytically separated its components. He pointed out that a cultural or belief system can be classified into four segments through two cross cutting principles of whether the beliefs are concerned with cognitive or evaluative ideas, and whether those ideas are empirically verifiable or not. According to the former principle, a cultural system can be broadly divided into those concerned with cognitive ideas and those which are evaluative ideas. For example, ideas about the formation of day and night, changes in climate, methods of control of human fertility, heaven and hell, supernatural creatures, and so on, are cognitive ideas. Distinct from these are evaluative ideas, which lay down the basis of evaluation, the basis of good and bad, beauty and ugliness, purity and pollution. It is on the basis of evaluative ideas that a particular social behaviour or social relation is preferred and another rejected. For example, for classifying food items, the criteria of purity-pollution may be relevant in one society, while in another society this principle may be irrelevant, and another principle of nutritive value may be dominant. The basis of human relations that is emphasised in one society may be achieved qualities like educational qualifications, while in another society it may be ascriptive attributes like caste and religion.

The other basis of classification of beliefs is whether they are empirically verifiable or not. There are beliefs like the shape of the earth, the formation of day and night, methods of control of human fertility, causes of misery, and so on, which are verifiable through scientific methods. In contrast, there are beliefs, such as those about gods and devils, and the effect of the supernatural on human affairs, which though form a part of cognitive beliefs, cannot be either proved or disproved through scientific methods. Similarly, while certain evaluative principles can be tested through the methods of empirical science, there are other ideas which cannot be either proved or disproved. Cognitive ideas which are empirically verifiable are called knowledge, and cognitive ideas which are not empirically verifiable are philosophical ideas. Evaluative ideas which are empirically verifiable may be categorised as ideology, while evaluative ideas which are empirically non-verifiable may be called religious ideas. The belief that one's material condition is dependent upon supernatural powers is non-verifiable, but the proposition that one's material condition is dependent upon one's caste can be verified by empirical methods. Even though at the analytical level it is possible to classify the totality of beliefs prevailing in a society into the four categories of knowledge, philosophy, ideology and religious ideas, at the empirical level, there is considerable overlapping between empirical and non-empirical, and between cognitive and evaluative ideas, making such a fourfold classification rather difficult. For example, the idea of purity, which is basically a religious idea, is closely related to the idea of cleanliness, which is basically an empirical idea. Because of such problems, for practical purposes, the belief system may be classified into the two broad categories of cognitive and evaluative ideas.

Talcott Parsons has also indicated that the components of a culture can be classified in relation to the type of motivational orientation that a person has in an interacting situation. The orientation of a person in an interacting situation has three dimensions, namely, cognitive, cathectic and evaluative. There are value standards for judging the relevance of an object in respect of each of these dimensions. Thus, the material characteristics of an object are defined in terms of cognitive standards, such as those about its dimensions, weight and colour. The appreciative standards lay down its appropriateness for the satisfaction of one's needs, and evaluative standards lay down the basis with reference to which the cognitive and appreciative standards are evaluated, and finally the object is treated as an acceptable or non-acceptable one. Since cognitive standards and appreciative standards are finally checked against evaluative standards, they provide the basic framework of value orientation. They constitute the genetic code of a cultural system, which patterns the various aspects of culture. This results in each cultural system developing and maintaining its own distinctive patterns. It also implies that even though there may be apparent variations in social actions at superficial levels, a commonality is likely to be found at the bottom of apparently divergent behaviour.

Culture is an autonomous component of social action, and has an existence of its own, independent of individuals and is external to them. However, as a child grows up in a society, it assimilates the various components of a culture, including its value orientation. Through this process of socialisation, culture becomes internal to the individual, a part of the personality, providing the framework for organising one's actions and expectations. This makes action in accordance with the values a need disposition or motivation for the individual. Thus, a cultural system, which is external to the individual, becomes a part of him, and becomes the basic motivating force for social action. Even though the organic needs of individuals, such as the need for food, sex and protection, are sources of motivation independent of the cultural system, the satisfaction of these needs takes place in accordance with the cultural values (Parsons et al., 1953; Parsons and Shills, 1959).

Culture and Development

The concept of development incorporates different dimensions reflected through different indicators. An important indicator of development is per capita income, which is determined both by the volume of production and the size of the population. It is basically a reflection of the level of productivity of an economy. Some of the other indicators of development are longevity of life, and mortality and fertility rates. Apart from these core indicators, there are other factors which contribute to the realisation of the central indicators, such as the productivity of various productive activities, level of literacy and education, condition of housing, water supply, environmental sanitation, and roads and communication. Such factors jointly contribute to a pattern of living, measured to fall at different levels of development.

A basic requirement for development is a strong desire in a large section of the society for an improved level of living, improvement in diet, improvement in physical well-being, improvement in housing and environmental sanitation, and freedom from diseases. To realise these goals, three essential requirements are: motivation for achieving improved well-being, knowledge for practising the particular pattern of life, and resources required to lead a life in accordance with the motivation and knowledge. Among these, generally the requirement of resources is well-known, not requiring further elaboration.

Knowledge is an important requirement for a better level of living. It has various dimensions. For example, for the effective utilisation of various flora and fauna in one's environment, one should have adequate knowledge about their characteristics. For maintaining good health, one should have some understanding of the importance of nutrition for health, and the nutritive value of different food items. In addition to knowledge, there should also be the motivation to make the best use of the flora and fauna in an environment. In many communities, such choices are made on the basis of non-rational values. For example, the ritual evaluation of food items in Indian villages has made many nutritionally valuable vegetarian and non-vegetarian food items non-consumable ones.

Improvement in housing facilities requires material resources. But one's aspiration about the type of house one should have is deeply influenced by social values. Knowledge and attitude exert great influence in the way in which one keeps one's house and environment. Keeping the house and its environment in a clean and tidy manner does not require much resources. It does not require much effort and expense for a household to dig a latrine and create a little privacy around it. Similarly, with a little effort one can keep oneself clean and tidy. The adoption of such practices is often influenced by knowledge about diseases caused through lack of environmental sanitation, lack of personal hygiene, and of motivation to keep one's house, environment, and person clean and tidy. Such an attitude is primarily a reflection of the underlying values about such matters. Knowledge about the importance of hygiene for health and of health hazards caused through insanitary environment motivates people to dig or construct latrines, and keep their surroundings clean. The lack of awareness about the importance of personal and environmental hygiene and the absence of cultural values emphasising cleanliness, apart from ritual purity, is an important reason for the extremely dirty appearance of Indian villagers and villages. Personal hygiene and environmental sanitation significantly reduce diseases and mortality rates and improve the well-being and longevity of life.

Attitude and knowledge also play important role in the efficiency of productive activities. For example, if a farmer has to obtain the best from his field, he should have a good knowledge of agronomic practices, characteristics of the soil, variations in climate, the characteristics of different varieties of plants, knowledge of diseases caused to plants and the methods of controlling them, knowledge about the effective use of fertiliser and insecticide, and so on. Information about post-harvest technology is also important. Knowledge about ways of protecting agricultural produce from rodents and techniques of preserving various agricultural produce would substantially contribute to the availability of agricultural produce throughout the year. Knowledge about various factors related to agricultural markets, such as awareness about the seasonal fluctuation of prices, and variations in the prices offered by different traders and markets, would contribute to the optimisation of farmers' incomes. It has been shown that improvements in marketing facilities contribute to increases in agricultural productivity and production (Von Oppen, Rao and Rao, 1985). Therefore, expansion in villagers' awareness and the level of knowledge about productive activities, production techniques, markets for various products, and so on, would go a long way in the more efficient use of rural resources and a better level of productivity. Knowledge is not only a proximate cause of economic development, but is an essential component for raising the productivity level beyond certain thresholds.

For optimising production and income, the motivation of the villagers to maximise output and income is an important requirement. Often, the peasant is subsistence oriented, basically trying to meet his domestic requirements. In such a situation, many peasants are not motivated to take up vocations and activities on the purely economic criteria of maximisation of income. As in other aspects of life, his choice in this respect is also influenced by social values. In Indian villages, ritual criteria are more important than economic return in the choice of occupations. The concept of ritual purity permeates all aspects of life—religious, social and economic—and defines all things, activities, and avocations as acceptable and non-acceptable ones. Because of its predominance, a variety of things and occupations are classified as polluting, beyond the purview of respectability and acceptance. For example, though hide is an extremely valuable resource, activities connected with it are unacceptable for most of the villagers, as it is defined as a polluting item. Similar values preclude a variety of activities like hogging and pisciculture, which are nutritionally relevant and economically rewarding.

Demographic factors play an important role in economic development. Improvement in diet, improvement in living conditions, improvement in environmental sanitation, improvement in medical facilities, and so on, lead to a reduction in mortality, resulting in a rapid increase in population, which neutralises the effect of much of economic growth, leaving per capita income static. Since the aspiration of the population at the early stage of development is to have a level of living close to subsistence, the voluntary effort for fertility control would be limited, resulting in a rapid increase in population living at the subsistence level. Generally, there is a long time-lag between decline in mortality rate and decline in fertility rate, and the establishment of an equilibrium between birth and death rates. As with other aspects of life, the desire for the number of children is greatly influenced by social values, such as the desire to have an improved level of living, the desire to have well-fed, and well-educated children, and the desire to be looked after by children in old age. It has been found from a number of studies that the number of children that a couple has is related to their perception of the ideal number of children that a couple should have (Mandelbaum, 1974). This, to a great extent, is based on social values.

Harvey Leibenstein (1957) has indicated that underdeveloped countries are in a quasi-equilibrium state, so far as increase in per capita income is concerned. When the income of a household in such a society increases, it does not lead to an increase in the consumption level of household members, as the consumption level itself is normatively set. Instead, the household may be utilising the additional resources on various other practices which enhance its status, such as having an additional wife, patronage of kith and kin, the elaborate celebration of feasts and festivals, and other practices symbolising its prosperity. Apart from such culturally set causes, increase in household income in the short run would result in reduction in mortality, and expansion in the household size. With such an increase in the size of the household, its per capita expense is pulled down to the subsistence level. An essential condition for a break from this vicious circle is the creation of aspiration for a better level of living, and the strong desire for goods and services associated with such a life, among the members of the community. Such an aspiration is the outcome of values about the ideal pattern of life prevailing in the society.

It took considerable time to understand the role of culture in socio-economic development. Max Weber (1952) was one of the first scholars who emphasised the role of ideas, particularly religious ideas, in economic action. He found that Protestant religious teachings, and the secular interests generated by it, substantially contributed to the development of the spirit of modern capitalism, like the rational pursuit of profit making, frugality and accumulation of wealth, rationalisation of economic activities and their pursuit for predominantly economic criteria, weakening of particularistic ties and the establishment of relations based on achievement, and the emergence of organisations giving priority to efficiency. The role of social values in economic development was further emphasised by David McClelland (1961). He and his colleagues were concerned with the fundamental impulse which produces economic growth and the source of this impulse. Their studies, spanning more than a hundred countries, indicated that variation in the economic growth of nations was closely related to variation in the psychological attribute of need for achievement (n'Ach) present among its members. The need for achievement motivated a person to do something better than it was done before, more efficiently, and more quickly, which contributed significantly to economic development. It was found that the main source of the need for achievement was the value orientation of the population, which was derived through the imaginative stories taught to children in their childhood. Nations with a higher need for achievement among its members developed faster. Florence R. Kluckhohn and Fred L. Strodtbeck (1961) in a comparative study of the value orientation and economic life of two Red Indian communities found that the community with more rational value orientation developed faster.

The importance of the cognitive aspect of culture, particularly knowledge, for economic development was emphasised by a number of scholars. Arthur Lewis (1957) pointed out that the accumulation of knowledge was an important proximate cause of economic growth. Technical knowledge about man and his relations with other men made significant contributions to development. Social knowledge was required for administering large organisations and creating institutions which favour economic effort, making social knowledge as important as knowledge of breeding new seeds or building bigger dams. Two important inventions which facilitated accumulation of knowledge were the invention of writing and the invention of scientific method. Literacy facilitated the accumulation of knowledge, and its retrieval, and vastly increased the potential for using knowledge in day-to-day work.

The importance of education, the main channel through which literacy spread, for economic development was emphasised by a number of other scholars as well. Frederick Harbison and Charles Myers (1964) brought to light the importance of education, and the resultant improvement in knowledge, skill and general capacity, on productivity and economic development. Their studies indicated a significant correlation between educational development and the economic development of nations. They emphasised that human resource was the ultimate basis of the wealth of nations, as it was the capability of people which led to the accumulation of capital, the exploitation of natural resources, and the building of social, economic and political organisations. This point was again stressed by Theodore Schultz (1963) by pointing out that the return on investment in education was much more than the return on investment on other items.

The importance of attitude and values for economic development was also emphasised by economists. Harvey Leibenstein (1978) emphasised that a transformation in the outlook of a significant proportion of people in the society from a traditional outlook, where economic actions were evaluated on non-economic criteria (like honorific and non-honorific, pure and impure), to an evaluation of them in economic terms (as those which gave more and less income, which made profit or loss), was an essential condition for economic development. Willingness to take risk and adopt non-traditional activities was also important. A psychological condition embedding such attitudes and motivations in the consciousness of a sufficiently large number of people was necessary for the stimulation and sustenance of development. Leibenstein also emphasised the importance of increase in the stock of knowledge and skills for development. These are qualities primarily created through value orientation and expansion in knowledge, giving a critical role for both dimensions of culture in economic development.

It was generally believed that the pursuit of self-interest was the main motivation for economic activities. But it was emphasised by Talcott Parsons (1963) that the motivation for the rational pursuit of economic activities was not based on the pursuit of self-interest alone. Economic motivation was not a category of motivation of the deeper level, but was a point at which different motives were brought to bear on a certain type of situation. Economic activities took place within the institutional or normative framework of the society, making economic behaviour an aspect of institutional behaviour. Institutional patterns were normative patterns, which defined what were proper, legitimate or expected modes of action in a given society. It was the normative pattern which set the goals of an individual's activities, as well as the means of realising the goals. The normative pattern prescribed the functions of every division of labour, defined role expectations, both positive and negative, and their evaluation. This made human activities, including occupational ones, and the motivations underlying them, relatively stable. As the norms were supported by the moral values of the society, the violation of norms, including those about the choice of occupations, created feelings of shame or guilt on the part of individuals and various forms of indignation from others. As moral values were deeply built into the structure of one's personality, adherence to these values was beyond the range of one's conscious decision and control. The question of what does one get through the realisation of economic goals was another important question, as economic resources were mainly the means to the realisation of further goals. Economic activities were propelled to the realisation of these goals. As was mentioned, these goals were not randomly selected, but were systematically ordered on the basis of the social values. As a result, the pursuit of economic goals, like the creation and accumulation of wealth, was done within the normative framework of the society.

The influence of norms and the underlying values in the pursuit of economic activities, in the selection of goals and the means of realising those goals, were profound. As the goals of life were set by social values, they determined the relative status of economic activities among the various activities performed in every day life. This requires a very high valuation of wealth for rapid economic development. It also requires normative sanction for the adoption of the most rational means of realising it. For example, the choice of occupations should mainly be on the basis of the income that one could derive from it. However, in a society where the generation of wealth occupied a subordinate status, and where occupations were evaluated on the basis of non-economic criteria, many of the potentially desirable economic activities were avoided, thus reducing the potentiality of economic growth. Thus, a value orientation pattern congenial for economic development accelerated the process of development.

Culture and Development in India

There have been efforts to explain the underdevelopment of India and other countries in Asia in terms of their culture, particularly their religious beliefs and practices. Max Weber (1958) believed that Hinduism adversely affected economic development. Those who stressed the adverse influence of religion on economic development emphasised the other-worldly and fatalistic orientation of the Indians. Based on his study of the influence of beliefs and values of Indians on economic development, Mishra (1962) indicated that belief in *karma* and rebirth retarded economic development. Following Mishra, William Kapp (1963) examined Hinduism as a religion and as a social system and its role in economic development. According to him, certain aspects of Hindu culture and religious values embedded in the social system acted as a major barrier to economic development. He particularly stressed the negative role of the doctorine of *karma*, and social institutions (like caste, joint family and kinship) in economic development.

However, there are scholars who found that Hinduism, and the Indian culture based on it, was not inimical to economic development. Milton Singer (1956) provided an interesting interpretation of traditional Indian culture and the values based on it for economic development. He pointed out that features of puritanism and asceticism co-existed in Indian culture, and contributed to economic development through the accumulation of capital and other means. Srinivas (1958) argued that Indian peasants were highly skilled and their activities were marked by practicality and earthliness. He attributed the failure of Indians to improve their material conditions to the social and political institutions of the country. Dube (1963; 1976) argued that traditional Indian culture has several elements that could encourage and stimulate economic growth, but structural inadequacies stood in the process of modernisation and development. He rejected the stereotype that Indians were other-worldly oriented. According to him, religious ideas institutionalised in social structure adversely affected economic development. Factors like caste solidarity, ritual obligations, joint family and kinship structures affected rational activities in pursuit of economic development. Tilman (1963) pointed out that the caste system stood in the way of economic development as it restricted social mobility. However, he also noted that values associated with caste had become flexible and had adapted to the changing socio-political contexts. Thomas A. Tinberg (1978) pointed out that Marwaris, in spite of their conservatism, were highly entrepreneurial businessmen. The case of the Nattukottai Chettiars of Tamil Nadu is similar (Narayanaswamy, 1981). Studies by C.P. Loomis and Z.K. Loomis (1964), Balwant Nevaskar (1971) and Bipin Chandra (1965) also refuted the Weberian thesis that Hinduism and Jainism adversely affected economic development. M.S.A. Rao (1969) pointed out that the Veerasaivas of Karnataka were puritanical, propogating that work was heaven, and tried to stimulate entrepreneurial spirit among its followers. These findings suggest that while there were elements of traditional values and institutions which could adversely affect the process of socio-economic development, there were also elements in the culture which could stimulate and sustain development. In such a context, the speed of development depended upon the extent to which the elements strengthening and weakening the development process were introduced into the culture and society.

Changes in Culture

Though culture is generally considered to be a stable component of a society, it has been recognised that it changed under the influence of various socio-economic factors. Daniel Lerner (1964) examined the process of modernisation in the Middle East and indicated that modernisation was associated with an increase in literacy, increase in media exposure, increase in per capita income, and political participation. The capacity to read, at first acquired by relatively few people, equipped them to perform the varied tasks required in the modernising society. Literacy was the basic personal skill that underlined the whole modernising sequence. With literacy, people acquired more than the simple skill of reading. The written word equipped men with a trans-personal memory. Man's activities and power were roughly extended in proportion to the increased use of written records. Literacy became the sociological pivot in the activation of psychic mobility. Thus, literacy and education, through which it spread, became the basic component in the transformation of the mental outlook of the members of a traditional society. Geographic mobility, urban contact and participation in mass media also were found to be associated with individual modernisation.

In a cross-cultural study of modernisation, Alex Inkles found that men changed in quite fundamental ways even after they reached adulthood and, therefore, no man needs to remain traditional in outlook and personality, merely because he was raised in a traditional setting. In the six countries studied by him, education was found to be the most powerful force shaping man's modernity. Occupational experience and exposure to mass media shared the second rank more or less equally. The city (urban influence) failed to qualify as an important independent modernising influence. Ethnic origin and religion also proved to be relatively unimportant. When men changed under the influence of modernising institutions, they did so by incorporating the norms implicit in such organisations into their own personality and by expressing those norms into their own attitudes, values and behaviour. It was emphasised by Inkles that neither could rapid economic development take place, nor could effective development be sustained without widespread diffusion in the rank and file of the population of those qualities which were characterised as that of modern man, namely, an informed participant citizen who was marked for some personal efficiency, who was independent and autonomous in his relations with traditional sources of influence, and who was relatively open-minded and cognitively flexible. As an informed participant citizen, the modern man identified with the newer, larger, entities of region and state, took an interest in public affairs, joined organisations keeping himself informed about major events in the news, and took part in the political process. His sense of efficacy was reflected in his belief that he might take actions which shaped the course of his life and that of his community, in his rejection of passivity, resignation and fatalism towards the course of life's events. He was independent of traditional sources of authority, like the village headman, priests, and parents. His openness to new experiences was reflected in his interest in technical innovation, his openness to scientific exploration of hitherto sacred or tabooed subjects, his readiness to meet strangers, and so on. The main thrust of individual modernity was to have more instrumental kinds of attitudes and behaviour. Inkles also found that the different aspects of the personality affected by contact with modernising institutions did not change in a random way relative to one another. The changes in one realm tended to be significantly related to changes in other realms in such a way as to create a modernity syndrome (Inkles and Smith, 1974).

In a series of comparative studies on the introduction of irrigation and the resultant agricultural development conducted in different parts of India, Alexander (1980) found that various dimensions of culture changed under the influence of agricultural development. In a study conducted in Sambalpur district (Orissa), in a block where irrigation was introduced through the Hirakud Irrigation Project, and in another block where irrigation was not available, it was found that beliefs and values were modern in the irrigated and agriculturally developed area. Beliefs and values of the respondents were studied through the O.M. (Overall Modernity) scale developed by Alex Inkles and David H. Smith. Responses to the 14 items in the O.M. scale were scored by giving a value of 0 for a response indicating a traditional belief and a value of 1 for a modern response. The mean scores obtained by the respondents on the scale from the non-irrigated and irrigated areas were 4.45 and 7.75, and they were found to be statistically significant at the 1 per cent level. This indicated that the process of economic development initiated through the introduction of irrigation also stimulated the process of modernisation.

Similar findings were found in a larger study conducted in Ganganagar district in Rajasthan where irrigation was introduced through the Rajasthan canal. This study was also conducted in irrigated and non-irrigated areas. It examined the values of 900 respondents from the two areas about agricultural and occupational practices, commercial activities and religion. It was found that agriculture and related activities were not perceived in entirely rational terms, as instrumental activities, but were evaluated on a ritualistic basis, and were conducted without coming into conflict with deeply cherished beliefs and values. Occupational values indicated considerable change in the pursuit of hereditary occupations and the segregation of those who follow polluting occupations. However, commercial values were primarily traditional and particularistic, with the expectation of obtaining favours from friends and relatives even in market transactions. Unknown persons were not trusted. Religious concepts like *dharma*, rebirth and the transgression of moral codes bringing retribution were followed strongly. Even though traditional beliefs and values were strongly held in both non-irrigated and irrigated areas, it was found that change in all the aspects of values studied (values about agricultural practices, occupation, commercial practices and religious beliefs) was significantly more in the irrigated area, indicating that economic development brought about through the introduction of canal irrigation changed, inter alia, value orientation as well (Alexander, 1982).

Alexander (1985) made another study of agricultural development and social transformation in Gulberga, Raichur in Karnataka and Bhatinda and Ludhiana in Punjab. In this study he examined the knowledge of the respondents from these four areas representing four stages of agricultural development in the country. It was found that the level of knowledge about natural phenomena, agricultural practices, elementary skills and values about occupations varied significantly with the level of agricultural development of an area. The level of knowledge increased and values became more rational with the level of development of an area. These findings indicate that culture, though a source of economic development, is also changed through the process of economic development.

Although cultural factors are an important stimulant of development, they are not the exclusive source of development. Therefore, the role of other variables like capital, technology, market and infrastructure in economic development cannot be ignored. For example, the introduction of irrigation, high-yielding variety plants, chemical fertilisers, and so on, substantially contribute to agricultural development. But the effectiveness of these resources can be more if social values encourage high productivity, high earnings, and the rational utilisation of resources. Culture being a component of a social system, including the production system, its pattern is likely to vary with the level of development of an area. The pattern of culture in a developed area is likely to be different from its pattern in an underdeveloped area. While the cultural pattern in the underdeveloped area is likely to be characterised by a low level of knowledge about various aspects of day-to-day life, and less economically rational values, those in developed areas are likely to be characterised by higher levels of knowledge and more rational values. This is the central hypothesis of this study. On this basis, it is argued that culture, being a component of the socio-economic system, tends to be in coherence with other components of the system. If other components are developed, like the introduction of irrigation facilities, high-yielding variety seeds, fertilisers, and so on, development would take place, but the inconsistent cultural factor would create frictions and resistance, through lack of knowledge to utilise the resources, and incongruent values. Though the development process itself would smoothen such incongruities, in the process, the speed of development is likely to be affected. Hence the need to bring about changes in culture in coherence with the requirements of development.

Methodology of the Study

As the main objective of this study was to understand the pattern of culture in areas with varying levels of development, a comparative approach was followed. Cognitive and evaluative ideas being the main components of culture, the aim was to understand their characteristics in areas with different levels of socio-economic development. Keeping this in view, three areas were purposively selected for the study—Azamgarh in eastern Uttar Pradesh, Saharanpur in western Uttar Pradesh, and Trichur in Kerala. The variations in the level of development of the three areas were strikingly evident from a variety of indicators, material and human, like roads, transport and other facilities available for visiting the areas, pattern of housing and the appearance of villages and the mode of dressing and cleanliness of the villagers. In each district, the study was conducted in a block—Phulpur block of Azamgarh, Rampur block of Saharanpur and Anthikadu block of Trichur.

From each block, a sample of 200 respondents was selected, through a two stage random sampling procedure. In the first stage, the villages in each block were serially numbered, and with the help of random numbers, 5 per cent of the villages were selected. The adult population in these villages was defined as the 'universe' of the study. They were listed with the help of the voters' list prepared for the 1981 general elections. A sample quota was allotted to each village, proportionate to the size of the adult population in each. These numbers were selected randomly from the list of the adult population of each village, and they formed the sample of the study. To obtain the necessary information, the respondents were interviewed with an interview schedule at their residence, by trained interviewers, between October 1984 and January 1985. Even though there were both males and females in the sample, the responses on behalf of the female respondents were given by the male household members.

From the selected respondents, three types of information was collected—details regarding their socio-economic status, details about their knowledge, and details of their values. The first comprised items of religion, varna, caste, age, education, occupation, father's education and occupation, educational level, main and subsidiary activities, and monthly earnings of the household members, ownership of land, type of tools used in production, details of livestock possession, details of the main crops cultivated, the cost of paddy production, cost of livestock production, monthly household income, spatial mobility, details and cost of dietary consumption, monthly household expenses on various items, details of household facilities and equipment, type and value of houses, types of vessels and fuel used for cooking, membership of associations, and exposure to various components of mass media. This information is used to create a picture of the socio-economic background and level of development of the three areas as also to derive a set of independent variables in terms of which the cognitive and evaluative dimensions of culture can be analysed.

In order to understand the pattern of knowledge prevailing in the three areas, the respondents were asked whether they had correct knowledge about various aspects of the following: characteristics of soils and plants, natural phenomena, elementary techniques, agronomic practices, livestock practices, nutrition and health matters, the cause of common diseases, fertility control methods, and philosophical and moral concerns. To understand value orientation, information was obtained on basic values, social values, human relations, agronomic practices, livestock practices, nutrition and health, fertility control, commercial activities, self-assessment, and aspiration for socio-economic advancement.

The respondents were asked a number of 'yes' or 'no' type of questions, dealing with various dimensions of day-to-day life, in order to understand their level of knowledge. For understanding value orientation, a number of value-loaded questions and statements dealing with various dimensions of value orientation were posed to the respondents, and their responses were obtained. The questions and statements used for understanding the knowledge and values of the respondents were finalised after pre-testing a preliminary questionnaire on a small group of 50 respondents selected from the three areas of the study. Questions and statements on which the positive/negative responses were within the range of 20 per cent and 80 per cent were retained for inclusion in the final questionnaire.

The aim here is to give a picture of the type of knowledge that respondents from the three areas have about various components of cognitive orientation. The percentage of respondents with knowledge about various items is given in tabular form and described. Further, the mean scores obtained by the respondents of an area on each component of knowledge were computed, by giving a score of 0 for a response indicating lack of knowledge and a score of 1 for a response indicating knowledge about an item. Through F tests and Tukey's HSD tests, it was inferred whether the variations among the means obtained by the respondents from the three areas were statistically significant or not. Apart from developing nine separate indices of cognitive orientation, an Aggregate Index of Cognitive Orientation was also developed by using the responses on all the 94 items contained in the nine individual components of cognitive orientation. Here, also, the scoring procedure was the same as in the case of the individual components, so that the score of a respondent could vary between 0 and 94.

A similar procedure was followed in scoring the responses reflecting respondents' value orientation. Based on the responses to each item in the 10 indices of value orientation, a descriptive account of the value orientation pattern was made. This was based on percentage analyses examining the percentage of respondents with modern value orientations. Indices of value orientation were developed by giving a score 0 for a response indicating belief in a traditional value, and a score of 1 for a response indicating belief in a modern value. However, the scoring patterns followed for the indices of self-assessment and aspiration for socio-economic advancement differed. In the former, the responses to self-assessment were placed on a 11 point scale, ranging from 0 to 10, and the responses to questions about aspiration for socio-economic advancement were placed on a 6 point scale, ranging from 0 to 5. The mean scores obtained by the respondents from the three areas on each of the indices was computed, and tested for the significance of inter-regional variations through the F test and Tukey's HSD test. There were 108 items in the 10 indices of value orientation, and utilising these items, an overall index of value orientation was also constructed. The ten indices of value orientation, the overall index of value orientation, the nine indices of cognitive orientation, and the aggregate index of cognitive orientation constituted the quantitative measures of the two dimensions of the dependent variables of cultural patterns studied in this work.

The influence of eight independent variables on the dependent variables was examined. These are father's education, education of self, membership of an association, exposure to mass media, spatial mobility, type of tools used for production, value of input used for the cultivation of paddy on one acre, and per capita household monthly income. The first 6 are social variables and the remaining 2 are economic variables. The social variables have been quantified in terms of scores for the purpose of regression analyses. For scoring the level of education of the respondents and their fathers, a four-point scale was used with a value of 1 for illiteracy, 2 for primary education, 3 for secondary education, and 4 for post-matric education. Respondents' membership in associations was studied by examining their membership in various types of associations, namely cooperative societies, farmers' associations, tenants' associations, labour unions, political parties, and socio-cultural organisations. A score value of 0 was given for lack of membership in any association, while a value of 1 was given for membership in one association. A maximum score of 6 could be achieved by a respondent with membership in all the six associations and a score of 0 by those with no membership in any of the associations.

Responses to exposure to mass media was examined in terms of frequency of listening to the radio, reading newspapers, seeing movies and visiting urban centres. Here the responses to each media has been placed on a five point scale ranging in value from 0 to 4. The scores given to listening to the radios was 0 for never listening, 1 for listening sometimes, 2 for listening occasionally, 3 for listening frequently, and 4 for listening everyday. The scores for reading newspapers were 0 for never reading, 1 for reading less than once a week, 2 for reading once in week, 3 for reading a few days in a week, and 4 for reading newspaper everyday. Watching films was scored by giving a value of 0, 1, 2, 3, and 4 for seeing pictures never, once or twice a year, 3–11 times a year, once or twice a month, and once or more a week. And visits to the town was scored by giving a value of 0 for never visiting a town during the previous one year, a value of 1 for visiting towns 1–9 times, a value of 2 for visiting towns 19–24 times, 3 for visiting 25–40 times and 4 for visiting towns everyday. The minimum and maximum scores that an informant could score on the four items of exposure to mass media ranged from 0 to 16.

Spatial mobility of the respondents has been studied by examining the frequency of their visit to various places outside the block, but within the district, in a month. The types of tools used for production were categorised into three groups—traditional, improved and power-operated tools. Those respondents who used traditional tools for production were given a value of 1, improved tools 2, and a value of 3 for the use of power-operated tools.

In this study, a descriptive account of the socio-economic characteristics of the respondents from the three areas and the type of knowledge and values held by them are first given. This is followed by an analysis of the variables related to the variation in knowledge and values, the inter-relation between knowledge and values, and the inter-relation among various types of values. The analyses of the variables associated with variations in knowledge and values are done through multiple regression analyses. Multiple regression analyses postulate a causal relationship between a dependent and one or more independent variables. In this analyses, it is assumed that a dependent variable is a linear function of independent variables. Therefore, through regression analyses, it is possible to estimate how much variation in the dependent variable (knowledge and value), is caused by the independent variables, separately and jointly. For the purpose of interpreting the data, the value of multiple R or R^2, the regression coefficients, the relative contribution of independent variables, and F values were computed. An important measure for the determination of the fitness of regression is R^2 and it gives the percentage of variance explained by the regression. It is a measure of how much effect a given change in the independent variable has on the dependent variable. The R^2 value gives the total variance explained by a set of independent variables taken together. For example, the R^2 value of 0.3723 indicates that 37.23 per cent of the variance in the dependent variable has been jointly explained by the independent variables together. The remaining variance, which is 62.77 per cent, is unaccounted and may be described as unexplained variation.

Multiple regression analyses give estimates of the relative contribution of each independent variable, and the contributions of all independent variables together. Where the independent variables do not explain cent per cent of the variation of the dependent variable, the contribution of each of the independent variables is limited to the portion of variance explained by that independent variable.

In a linear regression between two variables, the average unit of change in the dependent variable is associated with each unit of change in the independent variable. The regression coefficient indicates the strength of relation between each independent variable and the dependent variable in terms of this change. Depending upon the value of the strength (regression coefficients), it is estimated whether the contribution of the independent variable is significant or not.

Outline of the Study

In Chapters 2 and 3 that follow, the socio-economic characteristics of the respondents and the pattern of agricultural production in the three areas are given. This gives a picture of the socio-economic conditions in the three areas where the study was conducted. Chapters 4 and 5, respectively, give descriptive and comparative accounts of the patterns of knowledge and values prevailing in the three areas. While in Chapter 6 the relation between the socio-economic characteristics of respondents and the variations in their knowledge is examined, the subsequent chapter deals with the characteristics contributing to variation in values. In Chapter 8, the nature of relation between the pattern of knowledge and the pattern of values is examined. It also discusses the inter relation among various dimensions of values, and identifies the principal components of the values. The last chapter, besides giving a summary of the main findings of the study, also examines their practical implications.

2

Socio-Economic Background

In this chapter the salient characteristics of the respondents from Azamgarh, Saharanpur and Trichur are described in a comparative framework so as to give a picture of the relative level of development of these areas. This is based on information derived through interviews of the respondents.

Socio-Personal Characteristics

Religion and Caste: Among the respondents, 92 per cent from Azamgarh, 91 per cent from Saharanpur, and 88 per cent from Trichur were Hindus. Muslims constituted 8 per cent, 9 per cent and 5 per cent of the respondents, respectively, in the three areas. In Trichur, 7 per cent of the respondents were Christians. The caste-wise distribution of the respondents in the three areas showed that the Brahmins formed 3 per cent of the respondents in Azamgarh, 5 per cent in Saharanpur, and 3 per cent in Trichur; and Harijans 36 per cent, 38 per cent, and 12 per cent, respectively. The remaining belonged to the 'middle-level castes'.

Age and Sex: The average age of the respondents was 38 years in Azamgarh and Saharanpur, and 51 years in Trichur. As female members of the sample were responded by male members of their households, all respondents in the sample were males.

The average size of the households in Azamgarh, Saharanpur and Trichur was 8.0, 7.2 and 5.2 respectively. In Table 2.1, the

Table 2.1
Number and Percentage of Household Members Belonging to Different Age Groups

Age Group (Years)	Azamgarh (N = 200)	Saharanpur (N = 200)	Trichur (N = 200)
Babies	281	272	79
(0–5)	(18)	(19)	(8)
Children	260	211	86
(6–11)	(16)	(15)	(8)
Adolescents	180	216	141
(12–17)	(11)	(15)	(14)
Adults	826	632	636
(18–60)	(51)	(44)	(61)
Old	62	93	95
(61+)	(4)	(7)	(9)
Total	1,609	1,424	1,037
	(100)	(100)	(100)

Note: Figures in brackets indicate percentages.

number and percentage of household members belonging to different age groups are given. Children and babies formed 34 per cent of the household population in Azamgarh, 34 per cent in Saharanpur, and 16 per cent in Trichur; and adolescents 11 per cent, 15 per cent, and 14 per cent, respectively. Adults and old persons constituted 55 per cent of the household members in Azamgarh, 51 per cent in Saharanpur, and 70 per cent in Trichur. These figures indicate that in Trichur, there has been a sharp decline in the percentage of the population in the lower age group.

Education: The level of education of the respondents, and that of their fathers and household members was enquired. Among the fathers of the respondents, illiterates formed 82 per cent in Azamgarh, 74 per cent in Saharanpur, and 21 per cent in Trichur. Compared to this, among the respondents illiterates constituted 54 per cent, 40 per cent and 5 per cent in the three areas. A comparison of the illiteracy of fathers with that of the respondents indicates that illiteracy has declined by 28 per cent in Azamgarh, 34 per cent in Saharanpur, and 16 per cent in Trichur.

Among the respondents, those with primary education formed 26 per cent in Azamgarh, 25 per cent in Saharanpur, and 49 per cent in Trichur; middle and secondary level of education 15 per cent, 20 per cent and 38 per cent; and post-matric education 4 per cent, 15 per cent and 8 per cent.

The educational details of household members above six years are given in Table 2.2. Illiterates formed 67 per cent of household members in Azamgarh, 45 per cent in Saharanpur, and 6 per cent in Trichur. While those with primary education formed 18 per cent, 33 per cent and 37 per cent in the three areas, respectively, those with high school and higher levels of education formed 7 per cent, 10 per cent and 42 per cent in the three areas. With two-thirds of the population above six years illiterate, Azamgarh is a pre-literate society, a typical feature of an underdeveloped region.

Table 2.2

Percentage of Household Members Aged 6 Years and Above with Different Levels of Education

Level of Education	Azamgarh (N = 1,328)	Saharanpur (N = 1,152)	Trichur (N = 958)
Illiterate	67	45	6
Primary	18	33	37
Middle	8	12	15
High school	5	7	36
Post high school	2	3	6
Total	100	100	100

Landholding: The percentage of respondents according to size of landholding is given in Table 2.3. Those without any land, forming 2 per cent of the respondents, are the lowest in Trichur against 16 per cent in Azamgarh and 55 per cent in Saharanpur. The modal group owned 251–500 cents of land in Azamgarh; in Saharanpur 501–1,000 cents; and in Trichur 1–50 cents. The average landholding of the respondents was 195 cents in Azamgarh, 246 cents in Saharanpur and 49 cents in Trichur.

Occupation: In Table 2.4, the main occupation of the respondents and their fathers is given. Agriculture is the main occupation of both the respondents and their fathers in Azamgarh and Saharanpur. But in Trichur, the percentage of respondents in agriculture was only 12 per cent. While agricultural labour is the second main occupation in Azamgarh and Saharanpur, it is the main occupation in Trichur. Service and trade and business are other important

Table 2.3
Percentage of Respondents According to Size of Landholding

Landholding (Cents)	Azamgarh (N = 200)	Saharanpur (N = 200)	Trichur (N = 200)
Nil	16	55	2
1–50	13	4	72
51–100	22	4	12
101–250	22	10	12
251–500	23	10	2
501–1,000	3	12	0
1,001–2,000	1	5	0
2,000+	0	0	0
Total	100	100	100

Table 2.4
Percentage of Respondents and their Fathers in Different Occupations

Occupation	Azamgarh		Saharanpur		Trichur	
	Respondent (N = 200)	Father (N = 200)	Respondent (N = 200)	Father (N = 200)	Respondent (N = 200)	Father (N = 200)
1. Agriculture	63	79	48	53	12	21
2. Agricultural labour	13	8	24	31	25	35
3. Artisan	1	0	3	4	12	13
4. Trade/business	8	7	10	5	12	12
5. Service	11	3	11	3	17	9
6. Others	4	3	4	4	22	10
Total	100	100	100	100	100	100

occupations in which a significant proportion of the respondents are engaged. A comparison of the occupations followed by the respondents with those of their parents indicates a decline in the proportion engaged in agriculture, and an increase in the proportion engaged in agricultural labour and services.

Depending upon the nature of their activities, household members above six years of age were divided into workers and non-workers. Those who were engaged in any income-generating activity were defined as workers; those who were engaged in non-income-generating activities were defined as non-workers. In the household population above 6 years, non-workers and workers formed, respectively, 50 per cent and 50 per cent in Azamgarh; 66 per cent and 34 per cent in Saharanpur; and 67 per cent and 33 per cent in Trichur. The proportion of workers in the population tended to decline with the level of development of an area.

Among the 655 workers in Azamgarh, 77 per cent were engaged in the primary (agricultural) sector, 12 per cent in the secondary (manufacturing), and 11 per cent in the tertiary (service) sector. Among the 393 workers in Saharanpur, 75 per cent were in the primary, 10 per cent in the secondary, and 15 per cent in the tertiary sector. Among the 313 workers in Trichur, 45 per cent were in the primary sector, 10 per cent in the secondary sector, 45 per cent in the tertiary sector. These figures indicate that in a developed area, there has been a decline in the proportion of workers engaged in the primary sector, and an increase in the proportion of workers engaged in the secondary and tertiary sectors.

Earnings

Table 2.5 aims at understanding the incomes earned by workers belonging to different sex and age categories. In the 200 households in Azamgarh, there were 655 workers, giving on an average 3.3 workers per household. Compared to this, in the 200 households in Saharanpur, there were 393 workers, giving 2.0 workers per household; and in Trichur 1.6 workers per household. The reduction in the number of workers has been contributed by each category of workers. In the case of male adults, the average number declined from 2.0 in Azamgarh to 1.4 in Saharanpur and 1.3 in Trichur; those of female adults form 0.7 per household in Azamgarh, 0.2 in Saharanpur, and none in Trichur. The average number of male adolescents per household in the three areas were 0.3, 0.2 and 0.01; and that of female adolescents 0.3 in Azamgarh, and none in Saharanpur and Trichur. Children participated in the workforce only in Azamgarh, but not in Saharanpur and Trichur. Thus, with higher levels of development, there has been a decline in the number of people participating in the workforce. On the other hand, with the withdrawal from work first of male and female children, followed by male and female adolescents and finally of adult females, the proportion of male adults in the

Table 2.5

Number and Percentage of Workers According to Age and Sex and their Average Monthly Earnings

Category	Azamgarh				Saharanpur				Trichur			
	Workers		Average Earning		Workers		Average Earning		Workers		Average Earning	
	No.	Per-centage	Rs	Per-centage	No.	Per-centage	Rs	Per-centage	No.	Per-centage	Rs	Per-centage
Males												
Adults	406	62	213	38	288	73	710	41	250	80	450	52
Adolescents	56	9	116	20	34	9	326	19	8	3	190	22
Children	21	3	45	8	4	1	63	4	1	0	0	0
Females												
Adults	131	20	112	20	60	15	324	19	51	16	220	26
Adolescents	16	2	52	9	4	1	220	12	3	1	0	0
Children	25	4	28	5	3	1	97	5	0	0	0	0
Total	**655**	**100**	**566**	**100**	**393**	**100**	**1,740**	**100**	**313**	**100**	**860**	**100**

workforce has increased with economic development. Thus, while male adults constituted 62 per cent of the workforce in Azamgarh, they formed 73 per cent in Saharanpur and 80 per cent in Trichur.

The average earnings made by each category of workers in the three areas may be compared. The average monthly earning of a male adult is Rs 213 in Azamgarh, Rs 710 (233 per cent more) in Saharanpur, and Rs 450 (111 per cent more) in Trichur. The average monthly earnings of females increased from Rs 112 in Azamgarh to Rs 324 (189 per cent more) in Saharanpur, and Rs 220 (96 per cent more) in Trichur. The earnings of male and female adolescents and children are also higher in Trichur and the highest in Saharanpur.

In Table 2.6, the total earnings made by male and female adults, adolescents and children from the three areas, their percentage in relation to total household earnings, and the average earnings per household are given. The average monthly earning per household is Rs 550 in Azamgarh, Rs 1,181 in Saharanpur, and Rs 626 in Trichur. Compared to Azamgarh, household earning is 115 per cent more in Saharanpur and 14 per cent more in Trichur. It may be noted that the contributions of male and female children, and female adolescents to household earnings is negligible. The relative contribution of male adolescents declined from 6 per cent of household earnings in Azamgarh, to 5 per cent in Saharanpur, and 1 per cent in Trichur; and that of female adults from 13 per cent in Azamgarh, to 8 per cent in Saharanpur, and 9 per cent in Trichur. On the other hand, the contribution of male adults increased from 78 per cent of household earnings in Azamgarh, to 87 per cent in Saharanpur and 90 per cent in Trichur. These figures show that with development, there has been an increase in the relative share of male adults to household earnings, and decline in the contribution of other categories of household members.

Even though economic development resulted in increased earnings per worker, it has also led to a decline in the number of workers per household. As a result, total household earnings increased at a rate lower than the increase in the earnings per worker. For example, while the earning of a male adult in Saharanpur was 233 per cent more than in Azamgarh, the total household earning through male adults in Saharanpur was only 137 per cent more than the earnings made by male adults in Azamgarh. The total earnings made by female adults in Saharanpur was more by

Table 2.6
Contribution to Household Earnings by Different Categories
of Workers—Amount and Percentage

Worker Categories	Azamgarh (Rs)	Saharanpur (Rs)	Trichur (Rs)
Males			
Adults	86,324	204,508	112,385
	(78)	(87)	(90)
Adolescents	6,522	11,110	1,522
	(6)	(5)	(1)
Children	951	250	0
	(1)	(0)	
Females			
Adults	14,646	19,148	11,211
	(13)	(8)	(9)
Adolescents	834	881	0
	(1)	(0)	
Children	689	290	0
	(1)	(0)	
Total	109,966	236,187	125,118
	(100)	(100)	(100)
Average per household (Rs)	550	1,181	626
Average per capita (Rs)	69	164	120

Note: Figures in brackets indicate percentages.

31 per cent than in Azamgarh, though earning per female adult was more by 189 per cent. A more or less similar pattern was seen in the case of male and female adolescents and children as well. Consequently, household earnings in Saharanpur and Trichur were more by only 115 per cent and 14 per cent than in Azamgarh.

The average monthly household earnings was Rs 550 in Azamgarh, Rs 1,181 in Saharanpur and Rs 626 in Trichur. The average size of households in the three areas being 8.0, 7.2 and 5.2, the per capita earnings were Rs 69 in Azamgarh, Rs 164 in Saharanpur, and Rs 120 in Trichur. At the per capita level, income in Saharanpur was 138 per cent more than in Azamgarh, and 37 per cent more than in Trichur. Though household earnings in Trichur were considerably lower than in Saharanpur, per capita earning was only slightly lower, due to the smaller size of households in Trichur. Both in terms of household and per capita income, Azamgarh was the least developed, Saharanpur was the most developed, while Trichur occupied a middle position, closer to Saharanpur.

Income from Different Sources: Information was separately obtained on the income earned by the respondents from different sources in a month. In Table 2.7, the number of household members

Table 2.7
Number of Earners in Different Activities, their Monthly Earnings and their Relative Share

	Azamgarh		Saharanpur		Trichur	
	Earners (No.)	Earnings (Rs)	Earners (No.)	Earnings (Rs)	Earners (No.)	Earnings (Rs)
Total earnings from crops	148	69,761 (50)	85	125,297 (43)	62	23,085 (15)
Dairy	57	10,482 (7)	85	45,780 (16)	24	5,560 (4)
Poultry and livestock	29	2,007 (1)	4	35,804 (12)	9	395 (0)
Fishery/trapping	1	50 (0)	2	508 (0)	—	—
Household manufacturing	2	225 (0)	2	350 (0)	1	150 (0)
Trade/shop	35	12,055 (9)	35	2,000 (1)	25	10,185 (7)
Employment/service	53	32,005 (23)	50	51,065 (18)	102	76,639 (51)
Casual labour	52	10,753 (8)	59	21,114 (7)	52	21,860 (15)
Rent/investment	6	1,170 (1)	7	2,700 (1)	10	4,205 (3)
Others	22	2,000 (1)	15	4,400 (2)	30	7,924 (5)
Total	405	140,508 (100)	344	289,018 (100)	315	150,003 (100)
Earning per earner		347		840		476
Earning per household		703		1,445		750
Earning per capita		88		201		144

Note: Figures in brackets indicate percentages.

earning income from different sources, the total earnings made by them, and the relative contribution (percentage) of earnings from different sources are given. The total earnings of 200 households were Rs 140,508 in Azamgarh, Rs 289,018 in Saharanpur, and Rs 150,003 in Trichur. Compared to Azamgarh, household income is 106 per cent more in Saharanpur and 7 per cent more in Trichur. The earnings per household were Rs 703 in Azamgarh, Rs 1,445 in Saharanpur, and Rs 750 in Trichur. The earnings per earner were Rs 347 in Azamgarh, Rs 840 in Saharanpur and Rs 476 in Trichur. The earnings per capita were Rs 88, Rs 201 and Rs 144 in Azamgarh, Saharanpur and Trichur, respectively.

The main source of income in Azamgarh and Saharanpur was crop farming, respectively contributing 50 per cent and 43 per cent of the household income. Dairy activities contributed 7 per cent and 16 per cent of the household income in these two areas. On the other hand, the main source of income in Trichur was employment, contributing 51 per cent of the household income. Employment contributed 23 per cent of the household income in Azamgarh and 18 per cent in Saharanpur. In Trichur, the contributions of crop and dairy production were 15 per cent and 4 per cent, respectively, implying the relatively low status of agricultural activities in household earnings. Casual labour was an important source of income in all the areas, contributing 8 per cent of household earnings in Azamgarh, 7 per cent in Saharanpur and 15 per cent in Trichur. Household earnings from poultry, fisheries, household manufacturing, rent, and so on, were small in all these areas. The data indicate that while Azamgarh and Saharanpur are predominantly agrarian economies, Trichur has emerged as a non-agrarian economy.

Pattern of Living

Different aspects of life were examined for an understanding of the pattern of life of the people in the three areas. This included monthly household expenses, food consumption, type of vessels used for cooking, and type of house in which respondents lived.

Household Expenses: In Table 2.8, the average household expenses incurred by the 200 respondents in a month on different

Table 2.8
Item-wise Average Monthly Household Expenses

Item	Azamgarh (N = 200)	Saharanpur (N = 200)	Trichur (N = 200)
Food	355	327	499
	(65)	(49)	(75)
Cloth	72	121	63
	(13)	(18)	(9)
Medicine	43	41	47
	(7)	(6)	(5)
Religion	21	25	16
	(4)	(3)	(1)
Education	38	76	41
	(4)	(8)	(4)
Transport	27	53	31
	(3)	(7)	(3)
Entertainment	13	40	21
	(1)	(4)	(1)
Other items	24	54	98
	(3)	(5)	(2)
Average monthly household expense (Rs)	593	737	816
Average daily expense per household at the price level of Azamgarh	19.77	21.93	23.65
Per capita daily expenses at Azamgarh price level (Rs)	2.47	3.05	5.23

Note: Figures in brackets indicate percentages.

items is given. The table also gives the proportionate expense on various items. The average household expense in a month was Rs 593 in Azamgarh, Rs 737 in Saharanpur, and Rs 816 in Trichur, giving an average expense of Rs 19.77 in Azamgarh, Rs 24.57 in Saharanpur and Rs 27.20 in Trichur per day per household. However, as the size of households and the cost of living in the three areas varied, in order to understand the comparative level of living in the three areas, the per capita income at constant prices was computed. Since the cost of living index for the three areas was not available, the price of rice prevailing in each area was adopted as an index. The price of a kilogram of rice in October 1984 when the data were collected was Rs 2.51 in Azamgarh, Rs 2.80 in Saharanpur and Rs 2.88 in Trichur. The daily household expense in Saharanpur at the price level prevailing in Azamgarh was Rs 21.93, and in Trichur Rs 23.65. Dividing these with the average number of household numbers in the three areas (8.0, 7.2 and 5.2 persons), the per capita daily expenditure arrived at was Rs 2.47 in Azamgarh, Rs 3.05 in Saharanpur and Rs 4.55 in Trichur. Compared to Azamgarh, the per capita per day expense is 42 per cent more in Saharanpur, and 84 per cent more in Trichur.

The most important item of expense in all the areas is food. This accounted for 65 per cent of the expense in Azamgarh, 49 per cent in Saharanpur and 75 per cent in Trichur. Clothing accounted for 13 per cent, 18 per cent, and 9 per cent of the expense in the three areas; medicine 7 per cent, 6 per cent and 5 per cent; education 5 per cent, 8 per cent and 4 per cent. The exceptionally high expense on food in Trichur seems to be due to the high price of food items prevailing in Kerala.

Food Consumption: Information was obtained on the quantity of different food items consumed in the households of the respondents in a day. Utilising this information, the per capita consumption of food was computed and it is presented in Table 2.9. Cereals (rice and wheat) were the main food items consumed in all the three areas. Its consumption per capita was the highest in Azamgarh and the lowest in Trichur. However, the consumption of other items like pulses, vegetables, milk, and so on, was the highest in Saharanpur. The per capita consumption of almost all the food items, except non-vegetarian items, was the lowest in Trichur.

Household Utensils: Food was cooked in earthen vessels by 50 per cent of the households in Azamgarh, 7 per cent in Saharanpur, and 2 per cent in Trichur. The percentage of households using aluminium vessels was 44 in Azamgarh, 13 in Saharanpur and 83 in Trichur. The distribution of households using stainless steel vessels for cooking was 5 per cent in Azamgarh, 80 per cent in Saharanpur and 16 per cent in Trichur.

Food was cooked using cow-dung by more than two-thirds of the households in Azamgarh. But in Saharanpur and Trichur, agricultural wastes and wood were the main fuel. Households using

Table 2.9
Per Capita Daily Consumption of Different Food Items (in Kgs)

Item	Azamgarh (N = 200)	Saharanpur (N = 200)	Trichur (N = 200)
Rice	0.148	0.164	0.325
Wheat	0.231	0.230	0.028
Other cereals	0.096	0.016	0.007
Pulses	0.047	0.052	0.032
Vegetables	0.113	0.133	0.079
Milk and milk products	0.069	0.218	0.042
Tea/coffee	0.002	0.004	0.005
Sugar/jaggery	0.018	0.042	0.041
Oil	0.008	0.011	0.016
Egg/meat/fish	0.004	0.011	0.066
Other items	0.001	0.005	0.002

kerosene, gas or electricity for cooking formed 4 per cent in Azamgarh, 10 per cent in Saharanpur and 2 per cent in Trichur.

Type of House: The houses in which the respondents lived were categorised into *kacha* and *pucca*. Houses with mud-wall and thatch, and mud-wall and tiles were classified as *kacha* houses; and those with stone and brick walls, and a tile or concrete roof were classified as *pucca* houses. The percentage of respondents with *kacha* houses constituted 70 per cent in Azamgarh, 35 per cent in Saharanpur, and 75 per cent in Trichur. Conversely, those living in *pucca* houses constituted 29 per cent, 65 per cent, and 20 per cent, respectively, in the three areas. The percentage of respondents without a house of their own formed 1 per cent, 0 per cent, and 5 per cent respectively in the three areas.

Latrines were available in 12 per cent of the houses in Azamgarh, 32 per cent in Saharanpur and 73 per cent in Trichur, and bathrooms in 17 per cent, 38 per cent and 61 per cent of the households. It may be noted that even though people living in *kacha* houses were more in Trichur than in Saharanpur, households using toilet facilities were substantially more in Trichur.

The percentage of electrified houses was 57 per cent in Azamgarh, 41 per cent in Saharanpur and 55 per cent in Trichur. Radios were owned by 42 per cent, 60 per cent and 72 per cent of the households respectively in the three areas.

Summary

The foregoing analysis indicates that the socio-economic characteristics of the three areas differed. Azamgarh is a socially and economically underdeveloped area, characterised by a low level of education, large households, half of the population in younger age groups, larger participation of adult females, adolescents and children in the labour force, and low earnings per worker. Households derived the major portion of their income from the primary sector; the per capita expense was low; and food was cooked mainly in earthen vessels. People generally lived in *kacha* houses, which were devoid of latrines and bathrooms.

On the other hand, in Saharanpur the educational level of the respondents and members of their households was higher. About half of the population was 'young'; the participation of female adults, adolescents and children in the workforce was less; the earnings of all categories of workers was the highest. Households were dependent mainly upon the earnings of adult males. The major share of household income was from the primary sector. Household expense was the highest among the three areas. Most of the households cooked their food in stainless steel utensils, and a majority of the households lived in *pucca* houses, devoid of latrines and bathrooms. In Trichur, most of the people were literate, with a significant proportion having high school education. Though the average size of the landholding was the smallest among the three areas, those without land also were the least in Trichur. The proportion of 'young' persons in the population was the least. Non-agricultural activities have become the main source of income, and the major share of the income was derived from non-agricultural activities. The average earnings per worker was less than in Saharanpur, but more than in Azamgarh; most of the household earning was made by adult males. A majority of the households lived in *kacha* houses, but most of the houses had latrines and bathrooms. Food was cooked mainly in aluminium vessels. Though household earning was considerably lower than in Saharanpur, due to the small size of the household, the per capita difference in earnings was considerably lower. In short, the level of socio-economic development was the least in Azamgarh; economic development was the highest in Saharanpur; but social development was the highest in Trichur.

3

Pattern of Agricultural Production

In the previous chapter, a brief picture of the socio-economic background of the respondents from Azamgarh, Saharanpur and Trichur, and their way of life was given. It was seen that while Saharanpur had a higher level of economic development, social development was more in Trichur. In this chapter, the basic features of agricultural production in the three areas are examined. This involves, first, an examination of the material components of the agricultural production system, followed by the pattern of its organisation and its productivity.

Components of the Production System

Land: Land is the most important means of agricultural production. In Table 2.3, details of land owned by the respondents were given. Of the 200 respondents from each area, the landless constituted 16 per cent in Azamgarh, 55 per cent in Saharanpur, and 2 per cent in Trichur; marginal farmers (0.0–2.5 acres) 57 per cent, 19 per cent and 96 per cent; small farmers (2.51–5.00 acres) 28 per cent, 10 per cent and 2 per cent; and large farmers (more than 5 acres) 5 per cent, 18 per cent and nil, respectively, in the three areas. Greater equity in land distribution has been achieved in Trichur, where as much as 96 per cent of the households were marginal farmers. On the other hand, land distribution was the most iniquitious in Saharanpur, where the majority of the rural households were landless.

Information on the market value of the land owned by the respondents was obtained. The value of the 389 acres of land owned by the 168 respondents from Azamgarh was Rs 8,701,500, giving land the average value of Rs 22,352 per acre. The value of the 492 acres of land owned by 89 respondents in Saharanpur was Rs 12,873,443. The average price of land per acre was Rs 26,183. In Kerala, landholdings were relatively small, but land was highly priced. The value of 97 acres of land owned by the 196 respondents was Rs 12,477,120. The average price of land per acre was Rs 128,220. As a result of the very high price of land in Kerala, even those who just owned a house-site owned substantial wealth.

Fragmentation of landholdings was common in all the areas. The average size of landholding was 2.3 acres in Azamgarh, which was held on an average in 2.1 plots. In Saharanpur, the average holding of 5.4 acres was held in 3.5 plots. In Trichur, where landholdings were very small, there was 1.4 plots per landholder.

The average number of crops taken per field was 2.2 in Azamgarh, 2.4 in Saharanpur and 1.3 in Trichur.

Agricultural Tools: Tools are an important component of any production system, and they critically influence its efficiency. The type of tools used by the respondents were classified into human operated, animal operated, and power/oil operated tools, and their values were calculated. In Table 3.1, the total value of tools of each of these categories, and their average value per acre, are given. The value of the human operated tools per acre was the highest in Trichur (Rs 668), followed by Azamgarh (Rs 437) and Saharanpur (Rs 357). On the other hand, the value of animal operated tools was the highest in Saharanpur (Rs 541) and the lowest in Trichur (Rs 137). The use of power operated machines also was the highest in Saharanpur (Rs 4,819 per acre), followed by Trichur (Rs 2,873); it was the lowest in Azamgarh (Rs 2,032). The average value of the tools per acre was Rs 2,500 in Azamgarh, Rs 5,717 in Saharanpur and Rs 3,678 in Trichur, indicating that the intensity of the use of agricultural tools was the highest in Saharanpur. It was noted that power operated tools were relatively few in Trichur. Only 1 person owned a tubewell in Trichur, against 8 persons in Azamgarh and 17 in Saharanpur. Tractors were owned by 5 respondents in Azamgarh and 19 in Saharanpur, as against none in Trichur. The pattern of ownership of threshers, motor

Table 3.1
*Cost of Different Types of Agricultural Tools Owned by the Respondents
and Value of Tools per Acre*

Type of Tool	Azamgarh (Rs)	Saharanpur (Rs)	Trichur (Rs)
Total area	389	492	97
Human operated	170,007	175,859	64,808
	(437)	(357)	(668)
Animal operated	12,203	265,979	13,297
	(31)	(541)	(137)
Power operated	790,513	2,370,948	278,705
	(2,032)	(4,819)	(2,873)
Total	972,723	2,812,786	356,810
	(2,500)	(5,717)	(3,678)

Note: Figures in brackets indicate the value of tools per acre.

vehicles, and chaff-cutting machines in the three areas was similar.
In Trichur, the use of animal operated machines was also relatively
low. While ploughs were owned by 144 persons in Azamgarh and
80 persons in Saharanpur, they were owned by only 13 persons in
Trichur. However, the use of electric and diesel pumps have
become popular in Trichur, as compared to the other two areas.

Energy: An examination of the type of energy used for different
agricultural operations indicated that most of the agricultural
operations were carried on through human labour in all the areas.
However, the type of energy used for some of the operations
varied. For example, while in Azamgarh and Trichur, 32 and 36
per cent of the farmers prepared their fields using human labour,
in Saharanpur human labour was used to prepare the fields by only
a small proportion. As much as 47 per cent of the farmers used
inanimate energy for field preparation. The other operation where
mechanical energy was extensively used was irrigation—by 7 per
cent of the farmers in Azamgarh, 49 per cent in Saharanpur and 93
per cent in Trichur. Animals were used only in a limited way for
irrigation in all the areas. Irrigation was done through human
energy by 56 per cent of the farmers in Azamgarh and by 51 per
cent in Saharanpur. In Saharanpur, 52 per cent of the farmers used
mechanical power for threshing but, in Trichur, threshers were not
used at all. There, 98 per cent of the respondent farmers used

animals for threshing. In Azamgarh, threshing was done mainly with human energy. A number of other operations (like broadcasting of seeds, transplanting, weeding, spreading of manure, application of insecticides and harvesting) were carried out through human labour in all the areas.

Organisation of Agricultural Production

The cropping pattern in the three areas was not entirely similar. In Azamgarh and Saharanpur, paddy and wheat were the main crops, respectively, in the kharif and rabi seasons. A few farmers in both the areas also cultivated sugarcane and pulses. In Trichur, the main crops were coconut and paddy. Details of the number of farmers cultivating these crops, the area under cultivation of these crops, their yields, production, and related details are given in Table 3.2. The only crop cultivated in all the three areas was paddy.

Paddy was cultivated by 117 respondents in Azamgarh, 75 in Saharanpur and 42 in Trichur. The average yield of paddy per acre in the three areas was 9.4 quintals, 18.7 quintals, and 17.1 quintals, respectively. Compared to Saharanpur, the yield of paddy was 50 per cent less in Azamgarh, and 9 per cent less in Trichur. The production of paddy per farmer was 13.8 quintals in Azamgarh, 67.3 quintals in Saharanpur and 14.7 quintals in Trichur.

Wheat was the important crop cultivated during the rabi season in Azamgarh and Saharanpur. Its average yields were, respectively, 10 and 12 quintals in the two areas. The average production of wheat per farmer amounted to 14.2 quintals in Azamgarh and 31.8 quintals in Saharanpur.

Sugarcane was an annual crop cultivated by 93 respondent farmers over 49.0 acres in Azamgarh, and by 44 respondent farmers over 101.5 acres in Saharanpur. Its average yield was 10.3 tons per acre in Azamgarh and 26.6 tons per acre in Saharanpur. The average value of sugarcane per producer was Rs 1,625 in Azamgarh and Rs 11,958 in Saharanpur. In both these areas, pulses were another important crop.

In Trichur, the main crop after paddy was coconut. It was raised by 144 farmers in 44 acres. Coconut trees were generally grown in small plots, around people's houses.

Table 3.2
Number of Respondents Cultivating Different Crops

	Azamgarh				Saharanpur				Trichur	
	Paddy	Wheat	Sugarcane	Pulses	Paddy	Wheat	Sugarcane	Pulses	Paddy	Coconut
Number of respondents cultivating	117	154	93	97	75	86	44	18	42	144
Total area (acre)	172	218	59.08	32	270	228	101.5	33	35.50	44
Yield per acre (Q/N)	9.4	10	10.3	5.41	18.7	12	26.6	12.7	17.1	1,785
Total Production (Q/N)	1,617	2,180	609	176	5,049	2,736	2,713	4,197	616	78,540
Value of production (Rs)	280,426	418,775	151,160	63,189	619,998	479,825	526,149	93,039	104,038	220,000
Percentage of production sold	25	31	44	10	52	69	65	43	57	58
Amount realised through sale (Rs)	59,605	76,200	47,290	7,880	366,064	261,200	467,380	40,362	67,614	167,635
Cost of production (Rs)	548	526	590	205	862	818	1,290	398	1,699	1,385
Profit per acre (Rs)	655	752	1,191	617	1,147	871	2,153	1,691	1,220	3,290

Note: Q = quintal; N = number.

In Azamgarh, the major portion of agricultural production was domestically consumed, marketing being limited to 25 per cent of the paddy, 31 per cent of the wheat, 44 per cent of the sugarcane, and 10 per cent of the production of pluses. This makes agriculture in Azamgarh predominantly subsistence oriented. Compared to this, in Saharanpur, 52 per cent of the paddy, 69 per cent of the wheat, and 65 per cent of the sugarcane was marketed, indicating that there agriculture was market-oriented. In Saharanpur, the only produce which was predominantly used for domestic consumption was pulses. In Trichur, even though the average size of the farm, and the average production per farmer was small, 57 per cent of the paddy and 58 per cent of the coconut produced by the respondents was sold, indicating the market orientation of the farmers.

Cost of Inputs: For a comparative understanding of the cost of raising crops in the three areas, information was obtained on the cost of material and labour inputs used for the cultivation of 1 acre of paddy field by each of the respondents. This information was provided by 111 respondents from Azamgarh, 73 from Saharanpur, and 40 from Trichur. Utilising this information, the cost of 100 acres of paddy cultivation in each of the areas was computed, and these figures are given in Table 3.3. The total cost of cultivating 100 acres varied substantially in the three areas, being Rs 73,363 in Azamgarh, Rs 156,956 in Saharanpur and Rs 294,116 in Trichur. Compared to Azamgarh, the cost of cultivation was 114 per cent more in Saharanpur where the expense on every item was more than in Azamgarh. The cost incurred on seeds in Saharanpur was 66 per cent more than in Azamgarh; that on manure 25 per cent more; on fertiliser 86 per cent more; on insecticides 546 per cent more; on diesel and petrol 198 per cent more; on electricity 281 per cent more; and that on labour 167 per cent more. It should be noted that even though a certain level of mechanisation has taken place in Saharanpur, it has not replaced the use of human labour; but with the intensification of agriculture, there was a greater use of mechanical power as well as human labour. Agricultural development involved the absorption of more human labour and material inputs. It should also be noted that though there has been an increase in the value of all inputs used in Saharanpur, the relative increase was more in the case of 'modern inputs' like fertilisers,

Table 3.3
Value of Different Inputs Used for the Cultivation of Paddy Over 100 acres

Inputs	Azamgarh (N = 111)	Saharanpur (N = 73)	Trichur (N = 43)
Seeds	6,668	11,075	18,450
	(9)	(7)	(6)
Manure	16,222	20,436	18,475
	(22)	(13)	(6)
Fertiliser	22,070	41,026	37,933
	(30)	(26)	(13)
Insecticides	1,037	6,696	11,033
	(1)	(4)	(4)
Weedicides	—	2,159	—
		(2)	
Diesel/petrol	3,683	10,959	875
	(5)	(7)	(0)
Electricity	1,248	4,753	22,360
	(2)	(3)	(8)
Labour for all operations	22,435	59,852	184,990
	(31)	(38)	(63)
Total	73,363	156,956	294,116
	(100)	(100)	(100)

Note: Figures in brackets indicate percentage.

insecticides, diesel/petrol and electricity than in the case of seeds and manure. The 'modern' inputs were the products of scientific, high technology industries, and their increased use with development implied the absorption of modern, high technology into agricultural development.

Compared to Azamgarh, the value of almost all inputs used in agricultural production was more in Trichur. Two distinctive features which marked the use of agricultural inputs in Trichur were the non-utilisation of diesel and petrol, denoting that tractors, trucks, and so on, were not used in agricultural production, and the exceptionally large expense, in absolute and relative terms, on labour. Compared to an average expense on labour of Rs 224 incurred for the cultivation of an acre of paddy field in Azamgarh, and Rs 599 on the same in Saharanpur, an expense of Rs 1,850 was incurred in Trichur. Different causes have contributed to such heavy expense on labour in Trichur. It was seen that the extent of use of animal and power operated machines was relatively less in Trichur which necessitated the increased use of human labour. Secondly, wage rates in Trichur were several times higher than in Azamgarh and Saharanpur. As a result of such a huge expense on labour, the cost of cultivation in Trichur was 1.9 times more than in Saharanpur.

Livestock Production

Livestock production formed an integral part of agricultural production in all the three blocks. Cattle, buffalo, sheep/goats and poultry were the important livestock maintained by the respondents. Details of the number of respondents keeping different animals, and their number and value, are given in Table 3.4. It is seen from this table that large animals like cattle and buffaloes were owned in larger numbers in Azamgarh and Saharanpur. On the other hand, sheep, goats and poultry were kept in larger numbers in Trichur. The value of the livestock wealth of the respondents was Rs 556,211 in Azamgarh, Rs 1,065,794 in Saharanpur, and Rs 176,634 in Trichur. The average value of livestock assets per respondent was Rs 2,781 in Azamgarh, Rs 5,329 in Saharanpur, and Rs 883 in Trichur. Livestock wealth per household was the least in Trichur and the highest in Saharanpur.

The cost of maintaining the animals varied in the three areas. The average monthly cost of maintaining a cow was Rs 109 in Azamgarh, Rs 314 in Saharanpur and Rs 283 in Trichur; that of a female buffalo Rs 192, Rs 431 and Rs 284; and an ox Rs 158, Rs 251 and Rs 300, respectively.

The total income derived by the respondents through livestock in a month was Rs 55,357 in Azamgarh, Rs 133,075 in Saharanpur and Rs 31,656 in Trichur, giving an average monthly income of Rs 277, Rs 665 and Rs 158, per household respectively. Compared to Saharanpur, income per respondent from livestock was 59 per cent less in Azamgarh, and 43 per cent less in Trichur.

Summary

An analysis of the characteristics of agricultural production indicated that both crop and livestock production was the most developed in

Table 3.4
Details of Livestock Owned by Respondents

	Azamgarh	Saharanpur	Trichur
Number of Respondents owning Livestock			
Cow	92	103	45
Female buffalo	98	138	13
Male buffalo	15	60	—
Oxen	125	59	19
Sheep/goat	31	5	17
Poultry	33	4	35
Number of Animals Owned			
Cow	118	159	61
Female buffalo	136	218	15
Male buffalo	16	18	—
Oxen	209	109	22
Sheep/goat	81	22	126
Poultry	148	21	116
Value of Animals Owned (Rs)			
Cow	66,650	208,950	92,850
Female buffalo	253,150	618,199	32,701
Male buffalo	10,500	92,600	—
Oxen	210,151	141,450	22,800
Sheep/goat	12,950	4,300	25,895
Poultry	2,810	295	2,388
Total	556,211	1,065,794	176,634
Average value of livestock	2,781	5,329	883
Income			
All livestock items (Rs)	55,357	133,075	31,656
Average income per household from livestock (Rs)	277	665	158
Percentage of livestock product sold	36	27	59

Saharanpur, a little less developed in Trichur and the least developed in Azamgarh. While agricultural production in Saharanpur and Trichur was predominantly for marketing, in Azamgarh it continued to be subsistence oriented

4

Characteristics of
Empirical Knowledge

In the previous two chapters, the socio-economic characteristics of the respondents, the pattern of living, and the mode of agricultural production in the three areas was described. It was seen that living conditions were the least developed in Azamgarh and the most developed in Saharanpur, with Trichur occupying a position closer to Saharanpur. Efficiency of agricultural production also showed a similar pattern. While in this chapter the pattern of empirical knowledge prevailing in the three areas is examined, the next chapter deals with the characteristics of evaluative ideas.

The major component of cognitive belief is knowledge about empirical things and phenomena. For understanding the variation in knowledge, along with the variation in development, the level of empirical knowledge about the following were examined: natural phenomena; characteristics of soils and plants; agronomic practices; livestock practices; causation of diseases; nutritional practices; human fertility; technical knowledge and skills; and concern about philosophical and moral issues. The level of knowledge on these aspects prevailing in the three areas shall be seen.

Knowledge about Natural Phenomena

Knowledge about nature and variations in natural phenomena (like changes in climate and season, formation of day and night, solar and lunar eclipses) is necessary for the effective adaptation of man to nature, for carrying on agricultural and other activities in a rational manner, and also for a person to have a rational approach in dealing with variations in nature. For understanding the level of knowledge about natural phenomena prevailing among the respondents from the three areas, their knowledge about the cause of 13 natural phenomena was examined. These items and the percentage of respondents from the three areas with knowledge of these phenomena are given in Table 4.1. Item 1 tests the knowledge of the respondents about the cause of day and night. In Azamgarh only 4 per cent of the respondents knew about the rotation of earth and that it caused day and night. In comparison, 28 per cent of the respondents from Saharanpur and 66 per cent from Trichur knew this. The second item in the table shows the poor knowledge about the cause of wind prevailing in the three areas. Only a negligible proportion of respondents in Azamgarh (2 per cent) and Saharanpur (10 per cent) knew that wind is caused by heat expanding air. Even in Trichur, where education is widespread, only 40 per cent knew the answer.

Items 3, 4, 5 and 6 examine respondents' understanding of the phenomena of rain, climatic changes, monsoon, rain and lightning. Item 4 shows that those who knew the cause of climatic changes were just 4 per cent in Azamgarh, 18 per cent is Saharanpur and 38 per cent in Trichur. As a specific example of this, knowledge about the causation of the monsoon in July–August was enquired (Item 5). The response to this item also reflects the poor understanding of the cause of climatic changes. Those who knew the cause of the monsoon formed 11 per cent in Azamgarh, 13 per cent in Saharanpur and 29 per cent in Trichur. The process through which rain is formed was known to 17 per cent of the respondents in Azamgarh, 13 per cent in Saharanpur, and 75 per cent in Trichur; and the causation of lightning and thunder to 14 per cent, 33 per cent and 72 per cent in the three areas.

Item 7 shows that those who knew about gravity formed 14 per cent of the respondents in Azamgarh, 36 per cent in Saharanpur and 61 per cent in Trichur.

Items 8, 9, 10, 11 and 12 are concerned with solar and lunar phenomena, like the change in the shape of moon and solar and lunar eclipses, and the responses to these items reveal the poor understanding of them. Change in the size of the moon is an

Table 4.1

Percentage of Respondents with Knowledge about Different Natural Phenomena

Questions	Azamgarh (N = 200)	Saharanpur (N = 200)	Trichur (N = 200)
1. How is day and night formed?	4	28	66
2. How is wind formed?	2	10	40
3. How does rain occur?	17	13	75
4. How does the climate/season change?	4	18	38
5. Why does it rain in July–August?	11	13	29
6. How does lightning occur?	14	33	72
7. Why do things fall to the ground?	14	36	61
8. Why does the shape of the moon change?	5	20	40
9. How does the moon give light?	9	33	49
10. Does the sun move around the earth?	5	44	59
11. How does the solar eclipse occur?	4	22	35
12. How does the lunar eclipse occur?	4	18	33
13. How does a rainbow occur?	2	14	47

everyday phenomenon, and many village festivals and rituals are based on this. But the cause of this change is known to only 5 per cent of the respondents in Azamgarh, 20 per cent from Saharanpur, and 40 per cent from Trichur (Item 5). Item 11 shows that the cause of the solar eclipse is known to 4 per cent of the respondents in Azamgarh, 22 per cent in Saharanpur and 35 per cent in Trichur; and the cause of the lunar eclipse to 4, 18, and 33 per cent (Item 12). Those who know that the moon's light is a reflection of the sun's light constituted 9 per cent in Azamgarh, 33 per cent in Saharanpur and 49 per cent in Trichur (Item 9). Item 13 enquires about the cause of rainbows, and those with knowledge about it constituted 2 per cent in Azamgarh, 14 per cent in Saharanpur and 47 per cent in Trichur.

The foregoing examination indicates considerable variation in the level of knowledge about natural phenomena among the respondents from the three areas. For accurate comparison, the responses to the 13 items are scored, by giving a value of 0 for a response indicating lack of knowledge or wrong knowledge on an item, and a value of 1 for a response indicating knowledge about a phenomenon. The average scores obtained on the 13 items by the respondents are 0.92 in Azamgarh, 3.04 in Saharanpur, and 6.36 in

Trichur. The F test showed that the mean scores obtained by the respondents from the three areas differed significantly at the 1 per cent level: $F (2,597) = 360.81$. Tukey's honestly significant difference (HSD) test was used to find out the significance of intergroup difference between the means, and it also showed that the variation in the average scores obtained by the respondents was significant at the 1 per cent level. This means that the level of knowledge about natural phenomena prevailing in areas with different levels of development varies. The level of knowledge about natural phenomena is the least in the least developed area of Azamgarh, and the most in Trichur, where the level of socio-economic development is high, but not the highest. In Saharanpur, where economic development is the highest, the level of knowledge of the respondents is middle level. Thus, there is a certain degree of coherence between the socio-economic condition and this dimension of empirical knowledge.

Knowledge about Soil and Plants

Knowledge about the characteristics of the soil and plants is an important requirement for efficient agricultural production. For understanding the level of knowledge about this prevailing in the three areas, the respondents were asked nine questions. These questions and the percentage of respondents with knowledge of these matters are given in Table 4.2. Item 1 enquired whether the respondents knew that through chemical analysis the quality of the soil can be found, and on that basis appropriate agronomic practices can be adopted. Responses to this item show that 55 per cent of the respondents from Azamgarh, 79 per cent from Saharanpur and 81 per cent from Trichur knew of soil testing. Response to item 2 show that those who knew that loosening of the soil before the onset of a dry spell helps the preservation of moisture formed 7 per cent in Azamgarh, and 11 per cent in Saharanpur. However, this is widely known (81 per cent) in Trichur.

Items 3 to 9 enquired about respondents' knowledge : some of salient characteristics of plants. Items 3 and 4 show that most of the respondents knew that plants have life, and that plants breathe. Similarly most of the respondents (more than 80 per cent) in all the areas knew that sunlight is necessary for the growth of plants (Item

Table 4.2
Percentage of Respondents with Knowledge about the Characteristics of Soil and Plants

Questions	Azamgarh (N = 200)	Saharanpur (N = 200)	Trichur (N = 200)
1. Have you heard about chemical examination of the soil to determine its quality?	55	79	81
2. How does ploughing/tilling before a dry season help the crop?	7	11	81
3. Do plants have life?	89	80	100
4. Do plants breathe?	85	81	98
5. Through which side of its leaves do plants breathe?	6	23	10
6. Is sunlight necessary for the growth of plants?	83	81	97
7. How do roots absorb water?	18	27	31
8. How does a flower produce a seed (fruit)?	11	20	72
9. How plants produce food?	10	21	32

6). However, those who knew that plants breathe through the lower side of their leaves constituted a small proportion in all the areas: 6 per cent in Azamgarh, 23 per cent in Saharanpur, and 10 per cent in Trichur. Even though the importance of sunlight for the growth of plants is well-known, those who knew of photosynthesis were only 10 per cent in Azamgarh, 21 per cent in Saharanpur and 32 per cent in Trichur.

Item 7 enquires whether the respondents knew of the process of osmosis. Those who had some idea of it formed 18 per cent in Azamgarh, 27 per cent in Saharanpur and 31 per cent in Trichur. Those who knew of the process of pollination were 11 per cent, 20 per cent and 72 per cent, respectively, in the three areas (Item 8).

Responses to the nine items were scored according to the procedure followed earlier. The mean scores obtained by the respondents from the three areas were 3.62 in Azamgarh, 4.24 in Saharanpur and 5.97 in Trichur. The F value showed that the mean values among the areas differed significantly at the 1 per cent level: $F_{(2,597)} = 131$; $P < 0.01$. Computation of Tukey's HSD test also showed that variations in the mean values between the three areas differed significantly at the 1 per cent level. This means that there was significant difference in the level of knowledge about the characteristics of soil and plants prevailing in the three areas. Knowledge about these matters was significantly higher in Saharanpur than in Azamgarh, and higher in Trichur than in Saharanpur.

Knowledge of Agronomic Practices

The respondents were asked five questions to understand their level of knowledge about agronomic practices. These questions and the percentage of respondents with knowledge of these practices are given in Table 4.3. The responses show considerable awareness about various agronomic practices in the three areas. Item 1 enquires whether the respondents knew that transplantation of paddy seedlings gave higher yields than the broadcasting of seeds. This knowledge has become widespread in all the areas. The second and third questions are about the application of chemical fertilisers. Those who knew that it was better to fertilise the paddy crop at an early stage than at a later stage constituted 69 per cent of the respondents from Azamgarh, 38 per cent from Saharanpur and 80 per cent from Trichur. Those who knew that the application of chemical fertilisers did not adversely affect the quality of the soil formed 63 per cent, 54 per cent and 35 per cent respectively, in the three areas.

Items 4 and 5 enquire about the extent to which the respondents adopted some improved agronomic practices. Item 4 shows that 49 per cent of the respondents from Azamgarh and 62 per cent from Saharapur had tested the soil of their fields (Item 4). However, in Trichur only 15 per cent of respondents had conducted soil testing. High yielding variety (HYV) paddy or wheat was cultivated by 33 per cent in Azamgarh, 43 per cent in Saharanpur and 40 per cent in Trichur (Item 5).

The responses to the five items in Table 4.3 were scored according to the procedure described earlier. The average scores obtained by the respondents on the five items were 2.99 in Azamgarh, 2.78 in Saharanpur and 2.57 in Trichur. Thus, the level of knowledge about agronomic practices was more in-Azamgarh than in Saharanpur and Trichur. This seems to be due to the larger proportion of farmers among the respondents from Azamgarh, while in Saharanpur and Trichur the proportion of non-farmer respondents was

Table 4.3

Percentage of Respondents ·ith Knowledge of Agronomic Practices

Questions	Azamgarh (N = 200)	Saharanpur (N = 200)	Trichur (N = 200)
1. For higher yield, should paddy be transplanted or broadcasted?	86	80	88
2. Is it better to give fertiliser for the paddy crop at an early stage or at a later stage?	69	38	80
3. Would the application of chemical fertiliser adversely affect the quality of the soil?	63	54	35
4. Have you ever tried to understand the composition of the soil of your field?	49	62	15
5. Do you cultivate any HYV of paddy or wheat?	33	43	40

higher. The F ratio shows that the mean values among the blocks differed significantly at the 1 per cent level: $F(2,597) = 5.44$ $P < 0.01$. However, Tukey's HSD test shows that the variations in the mean values between Azamgarh and Saharanpur, and between Saharanpur and Trichur were not significant.

Knowledge about Livestock Practices

For understanding the level of knowledge of the respondents from the three areas about livestock practices, 12 questions were asked (Table 4.4). Among these, 5 were related to animals, 2 to poultry, 1 to bee-keeping, and four to pisciculture. The first question was whether animals have some degree of intelligence. Most of the respondents in all the areas knew that animals have intelligence. Items 2, 4 and 6 enquire about respondents' knowledge about modern practices of castration, artificial insemination and vaccination. Modern methods of castrating animals were known to 42 per cent of the respondents in Azamgarh, 73 per cent in Saharanpur and 47 per cent in Trichur. Knowledge about artificial insemination and control of diseases through vaccination was known to more than 90 per cent of the respondents in all the areas.

Item 3 enquires whether the respondents were aware that there was an optimum period within which a cow or a buffalo should be milked to get the best quantity of milk. This was known to 30 per cent of the Azamgarh respondents, 17 per cent from Saharanpur and 87 per cent from Trichur.

Items 6 and 7 were concerned with poultry farming. Hatching of eggs through incubators was known to more than 80 per cent of the respondents in the three areas. However, knowledge about high yielding varieties of hens was not so widespread. Those who could name at least one variety of high yielding poultry formed 17 per cent in Azamgarh, 49 per cent in Saharanpur, and 99 per cent in Trichur.

Item 8 is about apiculture. Those who knew of it formed 58 per cent in Azamgarh, 51 per cent in Saharanpur and 99 per cent in Trichur.

Items 9, 10, 11 and 12 enquired about respondents' knowledge about pisciculture. It was widely known in all the areas that fish could be raised in fish farms, and a majority of the respondents from the three areas had seen such farms also (Items 9 and 12). Items 10 and 11 show that though a majority of the respondents knew that fish breathe, the actual mechanism of fish getting air was known only to a small proportion of the respondents: 11 per cent in Azamgarh, 25 per cent in Saharanpur and 17 per cent in Trichur.

Responses to the 12 questions in Table 4.4 were scored as described earlier. The mean scores obtained by the respondents on the 12 items were 7.31 in Azamgarh, 8.15 in Saharanpur and 9.59 in Trichur. The F value shows that the mean values differ at the 1 per cent level of significance: $F_{(2,597)} = 105.41$ $P < 0.01$. The HSD test further shows that the variation in the mean values obtained by the respondents from the three areas was significant at the 1 per cent level. Thus, the level of knowledge about livestock activities among the respondents was the least in Azamgarh, higher in Saharanpur and the highest in Trichur.

Knowledge about Causation of Diseases

A healthy, disease-free life is desired by everybody. Knowledge of the cause of diseases helps one to prevent and control diseases

Table 4.4
Percentage of Respondents with Knowledge about Livestock Practices

Questions	Azamgarh (N = 200)	Saharanpur (N = 200)	Trichur (N = 200)
1. Do animals have some intelligence?	84	87	82
2. Do you know of any modern method of castrating a bull?	42	73	47
3. Do you know that there is a maximum time within which milking of animals should be done? If so, what is the maximum time?	30	17	87
4. Are you aware that cattle can be made pregnant through artificial insemination?	82	93	95
5. Is it possible to prevent animal diseases through vaccination?	83	90	96
6. Have you ever heard of hatching eggs with a machine?	83	88	97
7. Can you name an improved variety of hen?	17	49	99
8. Do you know that honey can be obtained by growing bees?	58	51	99
9. Have you ever heard that fish can be grown as cattle are grown?	83	86	95
10. Do fish breathe?	83	84	95
11. How do fish get air when they are in water?	11	25	17
12. Have you ever seen a fish farm?	77	69	58

through various measures. For understanding the level of knowledge of the respondents in this respect, their responses were sought on 17 items which, along with the percentage of those with the correct knowledge about the causes of diseases, are given in Table 4.5. Items 1–10 enquired whether the respondents knew the cause of diseases such as jaundice, cholera, malaria, typhoid, chicken pox, mumps, elephantiasis, tuberculosis, whooping cough and leprosy. These are contagious diseases, which can be prevented through appropriate measures. Responses to these items show the poor understanding of the respondents from all the areas about the cause of these diseases. Those who knew that jaundice is a water-borne disease constituted just 2 per cent in Azamgarh, and 10 per cent in Saharanpur; that cholera was caused through unhygienic

Table 4.5
Percentage of Respondents with Knowledge about the Cause of Diseases

Questions	Azamgarh (N = 200)	Saharanpur (N = 200)	Trichur (N = 200)
1. How is jaundice caused?	2	10	35
2. How is cholera caused?	9	6	45
3. How is malaria caused?	4	4	58
4. How is typhoid caused?	15	71	26
5. How is chicken-pox caused?	5	3	34
6. How are mumps caused?	3	3	23
7. How is elephantiasis caused?	1	5	67
8. How is tuberculosis caused?	8	1	42
9. How is whooping cough caused?	4	3	25
10. How is leprosy caused?	9	2	22
11. What is to be done to prevent smallpox?	26	62	79
12. What should be done if a rabid dog bites someone?	69	72	99
13. Is there any harm in drinking water from a village pond?	69	70	76
14. Is there any harm in villagers defecating in the open?	43	48	93
15. Is it more healthy to live in a house with many windows or one without any window?	56	62	95
16. Why are worms found in the excreta of some persons?	47	6	48
17. Why are worms found in the stomach of some persons?	45	11	47

water and food was known to only 9 per cent and 6 per cent of these respondents; that malaria is caused by mosquitoes was known to only 4 per cent of the respondents from both the areas; that typhoid is caused by unhygienic water and food was known to 15 per cent of the Azamgarh respondents, and 71 per cent of the Saharanpur respondents. The cause of airborne diseases like chicken pox, mumps, tuberculosis and whooping cough was equally unknown to most of the respondents from Azamgarh and Saharanpur. The cause of elephantiasis and leprosy was also unknown to most of the respondents from Azamgarh and Saharanpur. Compared to Azamgarh and Saharanpur, there was greater knowledge about the cause of various diseases in Trichur. Among the Trichur respondents, the cause of jaundice was known to 35 per cent; of cholera to 45 per cent; of malaria to 58 per cent; of typhoid to 26 per cent; of chicken pox to 34 per cent; of mumps to 23 per cent; of elephantiasis to 67 per cent; of tuberculosis to 42 per cent; of whooping cough to 25 per cent; and of leprosy to 22 per cent.

Items 11 and 12 enquired about the preventive measures to be taken against smallpox and hydrophobia. That smallpox can be prevented through vaccination was known to 26 per cent of the respondents in Azamgarh, 62 per cent in Saharanpur and 79 per cent in Trichur. The knowledge that one should take a preventive injection after being bitten by a rabid dog was very widely known: 69 per cent of the Azamgarh respondents, 72 per cent of the Saharanpur respondents, and 99 per cent of the Trichur respondents knew this (Item 12).

Items 13, 14, 15, 16 and 17 enquired about respondents' knowledge of common hygienic practices, for instance, that water in open ponds and defecating in open places may cause health hazards. Item 13 shows that 69 per cent of the Azamgarh respondents, 70 per cent from Saharanpur and 76 per cent from Trichur knew that drinking water from open wells may cause health hazards. In Indian villages, few households have latrines, and people generally defecate in open places. It was in this context that the question whether they were aware of the harmful effects of defecating in the open was made to them. Those who knew of the harmful effects of this practice constituted 43 per cent in Azamgarh, 48 per cent in Saharanpur and 93 per cent in Trichur. Ignorance of the health hazard caused by defecating in the open may be one of the reasons why 88 per cent of the Azamgarh respondents and 68 per cent of the Saharanpur households do not bother to construct latrines in their houses. On the other hand, the widespread knowledge about the health hazard caused by defecating in the open may have prompted households in Trichur to construct and use latrines extensively, even though more of them live in *kacha* houses.

Items 16 and 17 are also closely connected with knowledge about the importance of hygiene. Item 16 enquired whether the respondents knew that worms enter the stomach of persons, multiply there, and pass through their excreta. This information was known to about half the respondents in Azamgarh and Trichur, and 16 per cent of the respondents from Saharanpur. Item 17 also showed a similar trend. Responses to Item 15 showed that the importance of air circulation and ventilation was known to 56 per cent, 62 per cent and 95 per cent of respondents from Azamgarh, Saharanpur and Trichur, respectively.

The foregoing examination indicates considerable variation in the level of knowledge about the causes of diseases and awareness of hygienic practices in the three areas. Responses to the 17 items were scored, as earlier. The average scores obtained by the respondents on the 17 items were 4.10 in Azamgarh, 4.39 in Saharanpur and 9.21 in Trichur. The F ratio shows that the mean scores obtained by the respondents from the three areas differed significantly at the 1 per cent level: $F_{(2,597)} = 517.16$ $P < 0.01$. But Tukey's HSD test shows that the variation in the mean values obtained by the Azamgarh and Saharanpur respondents was not significant; but the difference in the mean values obtained by the respondents of Saharanpur and Trichur was significant at the 1 per cent level.

Knowledge About Nutrition

Knowledge about the nutritive value of different food items and related dietary practices contributes to a healthy life. To understand the level of knowledge of the respondents about dietary items and practices, eight questions were posed. These questions, and the percentage of respondents with knowledge about these items, are given in Table 4.6. The first item in the table enquired whether the respondents had some idea of the concept of balanced food. It was seen that the concept of balanced diet was known to 57 per cent of the respondents from Azamgarh, 67 per cent from Saharanpur and 85 per cent from Trichur.

Items 2, 3, 4 and 5 enquired whether the respondents knew of the nutritive value of some common food items. Lemon is an item of daily food, but those who knew that its main food value is vitamin C were a minority in all the areas, forming 27 per cent of the respondents in Azamgarh, and 23 per cent in Saharanpur and Trichur. Those who knew some of the sources of protein constituted 28 per cent, 45 per cent and 38 per cent in the three areas. Item 4 enquired whether the respondents knew the relation between the deficiency in the intake of vitamin A and night-blindness. Only 7 per cent of the respondents knew of this in Azamgarh, while 29 per

Table 4.6

Percentage of Respondents with Knowledge about Nutrition Practices

Questions	Azamgarh (N = 200)	Saharanpur (N = 200)	Trichur (N = 200)
1. Have you ever heard of the need to take a balanced diet?	57	67	85
2. What is the vitamin which occurs in great quantity in lemon?	27	23	23
3. Name the food which contains great quantities of protein?	28	45	38
4. Which vitamin is necessary to prevent blindness?	7	29	20
5. Is it better to use germinated pulse or ordinary pulse?	62	36	87
6. If one eats very large quantities of food, would it improve his health?	75	66	80
7. Can a child of less than six months be given rice?	17	30	47
8. The price of *ghee* is more than double that of oil. Does *ghee* contain double the nutritive value of oil?	74	32	67

cent in Saharanpur and 20 per cent in Trichur were aware of this fact.

When pulses are germinated, their nutritive value increases. This was known to 62 per cent of the Azamgarh respondents, 36 per cent of those from Saharanpur and 87 per cent from Trichur. Item 6 shows that 75 per cent, 66 per cent and 80 per cent of the respondents from the three areas knew that overeating did not contribute to better health. Item 8 shows that 74 per cent of the Azamgarh respondents, 32 per cent of those from Saharanpur and 67 per cent from Trichur knew that *ghee* does not contain nutritive items commensurate with its price. Item 7 enquired from the respondents whether a child of less than six months can be given solid food, like rice. This was known to 17 per cent, 30 per cent and 47 per cent of the respondents from the three areas, respectively.

Responses to the 8 items were scored as earlier. The average scores obtained by the respondents on the eight items were 3.45 in Azamgarh, 3.28 in Saharanpur and 4.44 in Trichur. The F ratio shows that the mean values among the blocks differed at the 1 per cent level of significance: F (2,592) = 38.6 P < 0.01. However, HSD tests show that the variation in the average scores obtained by the respondents from Azamgarh and Saharanpur was not significant; but the difference in the mean scores obtained by the respondents from Saharanpur and Trichur was significant at the 1 per cent level.

Knowledge About Fertility Control

The importance of fertility control for a better level of living was stressed earlier. For fertility control, one should have some knowledge about the biological processes related to human fertility, and the methods of controlling it. It was seen earlier that there was considerable variation in the fertility rate of the three areas, particularly between Azamgarh and Trichur. For understanding the level of knowledge about fertility control prevailing in the three areas, 12 questions were posed to the respondents. These 12 questions and the percentage of respondents from the three areas with knowledge about these items, are given in Table 4.7. Items 1 and 2 show that respondents with a rational understanding of the process of menses formed 27 per cent in Azamgarh, 9 per cent in Saharanpur and 44 per cent in Trichur. Those who had some idea of the period in the menses cycle when pregnancy is likely to occur formed 40 per cent, 12 per cent and 38 per cent, respectively, in the three areas. Those with correct knowledge about the life span of the sperm constituted 32 per cent, 4 per cent and 18 per cent in the three areas (Item 3).

Items 4 to 12 enquired about the knowledge of the respondents regarding various techniques for controlling fertility. That fertility can be controlled through the use of contraceptives was known to 68 per cent of the respondents from Azamgarh, 72 per cent from Saharanpur, and 97 per cent from Trichur (Item 4). However, Items 5 and 6 show that knowledge about the rhythm (safe period) method, and the female diaphragm method of fertility control are not so well-known. The former was known to 24 per cent, 45 per cent and 61 per cent of respondents, and the latter to 15 per cent, 38 per cent, and 69 per cent of respondents from the three areas, respectively. The loop method of fertility control was known to 33 per cent of the Azamgarh respondents, 50 per cent from Saharanpur

Table 4.7
Percentage of Respondents with Knowledge about Human Fertility

Questions	Azamgarh (N = 200)	Saharanpur (N = 200)	Trichur (N = 200)
1. Do you know why a woman menstruates?	27	9	44
2. Can you indicate roughly the period in the menses cycle when pregnancy is likely to occur?	40	12	38
3. How long is the active life of a man's sperm?	32	4	18
Do you know about the following methods of fertility control?			
4. Use of the male contraceptive?	68	72	97
5. Rhythm (safe period) method?	24	45	61
6. Diaphragm method?	15	38	69
7. IUD/loop?	33	50	95
8. Oral female pills?	62	54	93
9. Female sterilisation through tubectomy?	74	67	92
10. Female sterilisation through laparoscopy?	75	66	65
11. Male sterilisation through vasectomy?	73	75	95
12. Induced abortion?	27	41	89

and 95 per cent from Trichur. Those who knew about the use of pills for fertility control constituted 62 per cent, 54 per cent and 93 per cent of the respondents in the three areas. While 74 per cent, 67 per cent and 92 per cent of the respondents knew of tubectomy (Item 9), laparoscopy was known, respectively, to 75 per cent, 66 per cent and 65 per cent (Item 10). Vasectomy was known to 73 per cent of the respondents from Azamgarh, 75 per cent from Saharanpur and 95 per cent from Trichur (Item 11). Item 12 shows that those who were aware of legal sanction for abortion constituted 27 per cent, 41 per cent and 89 per cent of the respondents from the three areas.

The foregoing examination indicates considerable variation in the knowledge about the biological processes related to fertility, and the methods of controlling it in the three areas. Knowledge about these matters was particularly low in Azamgarh and Saharanpur. The techniques well-known among the respondents for fertility control were terminal methods like tubectomy, laparoscopy and vasectomy.

Responses to the 12 items were scored in accordance with the earlier procedure. The mean scores obtained by the respondents were 5.52 from Azamgarh, 5.37 from Saharanpur and 8.50 from Trichur. The F ratio shows that the mean values from the three areas differed significantly at the 1 per cent level: $F_{(2,597)} = 169.30 \; P < 0.01$. However, the HSD test shows that variations in the mean values between Azamgarh and Saharanpur was not significant; but that between Azamgarh and Trichur, and between Saharanpur and Trichur was significant. This means that while respondents from Azamgarh and Saharanpur have more or less similar levels of knowledge about fertility control methods, the level of knowledge of respondents from Trichur is higher. This is in conformity with the earlier finding that while Azamgarh and Saharanpur have a similar level of fertility, it is considerably less in Trichur.

Technical Knowledge and Skill

Information was also obtained on elementary technical knowledge and skill prevailing among the respondents. The questions asked for this purpose and the percentage of respondents with knowledge about these matters is given in Table 4.8. The first three questions enquired whether the respondents knew how diesel and petrol engines, electric motors and steam engines worked. Those who knew the mechanism of the working of diesel and petrol engines formed 6 per cent, 15 per cent and 24 per cent in the three areas, respectively. The proportion of the respondents with knowledge of the working of electric motors and steam engines was almost similar.

Item 4 shows that the principle of floatation was known only to 4 per cent of the respondents in Azamgarh, 3 per cent in Saharanpur and 24 per cent in Trichur. Item 7 was a related one—and it showed that those who knew the reason why it is easier to pull a thing in water was 21 per cent in Azamgarh, 6 per cent in Saharanpur and 40 per cent in Trichur.

Table 4.8
Percentage of Respondents with Elementary Technical Knowledge and Skills

Questions	Azamgarh (N = 200)	Saharanpur (N = 200)	Trichur (N = 200)
Do you know the following?			
1. How a diesel/petrol engine works?	6	15	24
2. How an electric motor works?	6	19	25
3. How a steam engine works?	8	17	25
4. How an iron boat floats in water?	4	3	24
5. For heavy tilling, is a spade with a long or short handle desirable?	69	41	89
6. On village roads, is it easier to ply a bullock-cart with a large wheel or a small wheel?	39	51	84
7. Why is it easier to pull something under water than over soil?	21	6	40
8. Have you seen a pulley used for drawing water from a well?	91	90	95
9. Have you ever travelled by train?	95	89	87
10. Do you know how to ride a bicycle?	81	81	71
11. Do you know how to write?	54	64	92
12. Do you know the division of numbers?	41	63	88
13. Do you know driving?	14	32	20
14. Do you know tieing electric fuse wire?	19	48	49
15. Do you know how to light a petromax?	23	50	66

Item 5 enquired whether a spade with a long or short handle was efficient for heavy tilling of the soil. Those who knew that a spade with a longer handle was more efficient for this purpose formed 69 per cent of the respondents from Azamgarh, 41 per cent from Saharanpur and 89 per cent from Trichur. Those who knew that a cart with a larger wheel was more efficient on village roads formed 39 per cent, 51 per cent and 84 per cent in the three areas (Item 6).

Items 8, 9 and 10 enquired whether the respondents were aware of some simple equipments which made work easier. Most of the respondents had seen pulleys used for drawing water, had travelled by train, and knew how to cycle. Writing was known to 54 per cent of the respondents from Azamgarh, 64 per cent from Saharanpur and 92 per cent from Trichur. The division of numbers was known to 41 per cent, 63 per cent and 88 per cent of the respondents from the three areas.

Items 13, 14 and 15 enquired whether respondents knew some mechanical skills. Driving was known to 14 per cent of the Azamgarh respondents, 32 per cent from Saharanpur and 20 per cent from Trichur; the tieing of electric fuse wire to 19 per cent, 48 per cent and 49 per cent; and lighting a petromax to 23 per cent, 50 per cent and 66 per cent. These responses indicate that as in other aspects of empirical knowledge, the elementary technical skills of the respondents from the three areas also vary.

Responses to the 15 items were scored according to the procedure described earlier. The mean scores obtained by the respondents were 5.67 in Azamgarh, 6.71 in Saharanpur and 8.70 in Trichur. The F ratio shows that the variations among the mean values were significant at the 1 per cent level of significance: $F(2,597) = 130.01$ P < 0.01. The HSD test also showed that the variations among the mean values were significant at the 1 per cent level.

Concern About Philosophical and Moral Issues

Though most of the people were mainly concerned about the problems of day-to-day living, they were also concerned with broader philosophical issues like the creation of the earth and the purpose of human existence. In this section, three issues pertaining to philosophical and moral aspects have been enquired from the respondents. The questions asked in this connection and the percentage of respondents whose responses indicated such concern are given in Table 4.9. Item 1 in the table shows that those who were concerned about the problem of how the earth was created formed 14 per cent of respondents from Azamgarh, 17 per cent from Saharanpur and 45 per cent from Trichur. Those who thought of how the world and living beings came into existence formed 17 per cent of respondents from Azamgarh and Saharanpur and 47 per cent of the Trichur respondents (Item 2). The respondents who were concerned about the rationale behind human sufferings and prosperity formed 35 per cent, 26 per cent and 47 per cent, respectively, in the three areas.

The mean scores obtained by the respondents on the three items are 0.65 in Azamgarh, 0.60 in Saharanpur and 1.38 in Trichur. The

Table 4.9
Percentage of Respondents Concerned about Philosophical/Moral Issues

Items	Azamgarh (N = 200)	Saharanpur (N = 200)	Trichur (N = 200)
1. Were you ever concerned with the problem of how the earth was created? (Yes)	14	17	45
2. Have you ever thought how this world and living beings came into existence? (Yes)	17	17	47
3. Have you ever thought why some people suffer a lot in life, while others are prosperous? (Yes)	35	26	47

value of the F ratio shows that the mean scores differed significantly at the 1 per cent level: $F (2,597) = 26.84$ $P < 0.01$. The HSD test showed that the mean values between Azamgarh and Saharanpur did not show any significant difference. However, the mean values between Saharanpur and Trichur and Trichur and Azamgarh showed significant difference at the 1 per cent.

Summary

In this chapter, eight aspects of the empirical knowledge of the respondents from Azamgarh, Saharanpur and Trichur and their concern with philosophical and moral issues were examined. The analysis shows that there is marked variation in the level of empirical knowledge prevailing in the three areas. By and large, the level of knowledge is less in Azamgarh, more in Saharanpur and the highest in Trichur. On certain aspects of knowledge, such as about health and hygiene and fertility control, the level of knowledge among the Azamgarh and Saharanpur respondents was not high. The level of technical knowledge and skill varies in the three areas, it being the lowest in Azamgarh, the least developed area, and the highest in Trichur, a developed area. Thus, a congruence is seen between the level of socio-economic development of an area and the level of empirical knowledge prevailing in the population of that area.

5

Characteristics of Value Orientation

In the previous chapter, the pattern of empirical knowledge prevailing in areas of varying socio-economic development was examined. In this chapter, the type of social values prevailing in the three areas will be examined by studying the following aspects of value orientation: basic values, social values, values about human relations, values about agronomic practices, values about livestock farming, values about nutrition and health, values about fertility control practices, values about commercial activities, aspiration for socio-economic advancement, and self-assessment. The hypothesis is that the pattern of value orientation being a component of the socio-economic system, values in underdeveloped areas are likely to be conservative, while values in the developed areas are likely to be more rational and modern.

Basic Values

Basic values are those values with reference to which other values are evaluated, constituting the moral foundation of society. By providing the basic framework of evaluation, the moral values colour all aspects of social action. In order to understand the nature of the basic values followed by the respondents, their responses were obtained on 11 items. These items and the percentage of the respondents whose responses indicated modern values are given in Table 5.1. Item 1 enquired about the way in

Table 5.1

Statements Used for Understanding the Basic Values and Percentage of Respondents with Rational/Modern Values

Statements	Azamgarh (N = 200)	Saharanpur (N = 200)	Trichur (N = 200)
1. People will have different goals in their life. Some people say that one's main concern in life should be to enjoy life. Some others say that one's main concern in life should be to achieve salvation. How do you describe the goal of your life? (Enjoy life)	49	45	53
2. There are some people who in their anxiety to achieve positions and accumulate wealth, do not care to observe customary values and obligations, such as living with their parents and taking care of them. Do you approve of their behaviour? (Yes)	45	48	85
3. What is important in life? Is it to be satisfied with one's condition, or to work hard to achieve more? (Work hard)	70	69	84
4. Do you think that the observance of our forefathers' customs and practices is necessary? (No)	37	34	36
5. Do you think that God will punish those who break established traditional customs and practices? (No)	63	40	72
6. Do you agree with the saying that man may propose many things, but it is God who decides the outcome? (No)	34	29	42
7. It may be possible for a criminal to escape from the law, but not from the hands of God. (No)	21	27	22
8. Can a person who does not believe in God be a good person? (Yes)	30	49	28
9. Do you think that every event in a person's life is already determined by fate? (No)	34	29	50
10. Do you think that a saint can perform miracles? (No)	50	61	89
11. Do you believe that there are ghosts and evil spirits? (No)	55	67	88

Note: Responses considered rational/modern are in barackets.

which respondents perceived the purpose of their life—whether it was to enjoy life, or to work for the realisation of salvation. The response to this item showed that 49 per cent of the respondents from Azamgarh, 45 per cent from Saharanpur and 53 per cent from Trichur gave priority to the spiritual ends of life. However, as Item 3 shows, this does not mean inaction. It is believed by 70 per cent of the Azamgarh respondents, 69 per cent from Saharanpur and 84 per cent from Trichur, that one may not be satisfied with one's condition, but may continue to work hard to achieve more.

Items 2, 4 and 5 enquired into the extent to which the respondents felt it desirable to observe traditional customs and practices. Adherence to traditional customs is believed to be one's moral responsibility, one's *dharma*. Looking after parents in their old age is strongly believed to be one's responsibility. But spatial and occupational mobility necessitates one to be away from one's parents, so one is unable to take personal care of them in their difficulties. Response to Item 2 indicated that such a value continues to be widely held in all the areas. Those who approved of breaking traditional custom in this respect formed 45 per cent in Azamgarh, 48 per cent in Saharanpur and 85 per cent in Trichur.

Item 4 enquired whether 'the respondents felt it necessary to observe the customs and practices of their ancestors. A majority of the respondents in all the areas placed value on doing so. Those who believed that it was not necessary to do so formed 37 per cent in Azamgarh, 34 per cent in Saharanpur, and 36 per cent in Trichur. However, those who believed that breaking of the customary practices may not bring about supernatural sanctions formed 63 per cent in Azamgarh, 40 per cent in Saharanpur and 72 per cent in Trichur (Item 5).

Items 6, 7 and 9 enquired about the different dimensions of fate believed by the respondents. Response to Items 6, 7 and 9 indicated the great belief of the respondents that an individual's destiny is predetermined. Those who do not believe in the saying that 'man proposes, but God disposes,' formed 34 per cent of the respondents in Azamgarh, 27 per cent in Saharanpur and 42 per cent in Trichur (Item 6). The strong belief that a person cannot avoid receiving the retribution of the supernatural is reflected by Item 7. Those who do not believe in such retribution form 21 per cent of the respondents in Azamgarh, 27 per cent in Saharanpur and 22 per cent in Trichur. Item 9 reflects the strong belief of the respondents that every event in a person's life is already determined by fate. It leaves an individual with little option to determine his own destiny.

Item 8 enquired whether the respondents perceived an identity between religion and morality. The question is whether a non-religious man can be a good person. Respondents strongly identified between religion and moral uprightness.

There is considerable ambiguity on the part of respondents to the question whether they believed that a saint could perform miracles (Item 10). Those who did not believe it formed 50 per cent in Azamgarh, 61 per cent in Saharanpur and 89 per cent in Kerala. Item 11 indicated that a majority of the respondents did not believe in the existence of ghosts and evil spirits, their percentage being 55 per cent in Azamgarh, 67 per cent in Saharanpur and 88 per cent in Trichur.

An examination of the basic values of the respondents from the three areas reflect their strong belief that salvation of the soul is more important than enjoyment of life. There is strong valuation on conformity to traditional practices. Fatalism is widespread and human fortune is believed to be under supernatural control. Nevertheless, there is also the belief that one should work hard for material achievements.

Responses to the 11 items were scored as earlier, by giving a score value of 0 for a response indicating belief in a traditional value, and a score of 1 for a response indicating belief in a modern value. The average scores obtained by the respondents on the 11 items were 4.93 in Azamgarh, 5.01 in Saharanpur and 5.78 in Trichur. The value of F shows that the mean values among the three areas differed significantly at the 1 per cent level.

Social Values

Information was obtained on the nature of social values held by the respondents. For this purpose, their responses were sought on 22 statements, enquiring about the nature of values held by them on different aspects of day-to-day life, such as inter-family relations, basis of employment, commercial transactions, inter-personal relations, punctuality and desire for material possessions. The 22 statements and the percentage of respondents with modern social values in these aspects of life are given in Table 5.2.

Table 5.2
Statements Used for Understanding Social Values and the Percentage
of Respondents with Modern Values

Statements	Azamgarh (N = 200)	Saharanpur (N = 200)	Trichur (N = 200)
1. If a villager wins a lottery, should he share the money with his brother? (No)	23	32	48
2. Should a person working and living with his family elsewhere, send money to his brothers who are in the village? (No)	16	28	38
3. Is it desirable for farmers to get their work done by several farmers working together, or is it desirable to get the work done by employing labourers? (Employing labourers)	16	53	71
4. When there are educated unemployed youths in an area, is it desirable for a factory owner to employ persons from other areas who are more efficient? (Yes)	40	45	49
5. Should a person selling his house make the sale only to persons belonging to his own caste, who generally live together, or to whosoever pays the highest price? (Highest price)	68	69	90
6. Is it desirable to allow Harijans to worship in village temples? (Yes)	76	73	95
7. On occasions such as the celebration of Dussera/Onam/etc., is it preferable to have groups of persons belonging to different castes formed for celebration? Or to have these groups made of persons belonging to the same caste? (Different castes)	84	70	78
8. Whom would you prefer as a business partner? A close relative? Or anybody who has the necessary finance and technical knowledge? (Finance and knowledge)	60	67	87
9. Is it appropriate for a Harijan to sit next to a Brahmin in a bus? (Yes)	72	70	96
10. Is it appropriate for a village tea shop owner to serve food to a Brahmin customer and a Harijan customer on the same table in his shop? (Yes)	80	70	98

Table 5.2 (Continued)

Statements	Azamgarh (N = 200)	Saharanpur (N = 200)	Trichur (N = 200)
11. These days, agricultural labourers in many places demand increased wages from the farmers; but in the past they were satisfied with what was paid to them. Which practice, you think, is the appropriate one? (Demand wage)	56	71	90
12. It is through their hard work and frugality that the rich have accumulated wealth. As such, is it desirable to take away a part of their wealtn through taxes, and use it for the benefit of the poor? (Yes)	66	76	91
13. Is it necessary for a clerk to stand up when an officer talks to him? (No)	40	44	19
14. A school starts at 10 a.m. and students coming late are punished. As children have to walk long distances to reach the school, is it desirable to punish those who come late? (Yes)	59	52	74
15. Two friends agreed to meet at the bus stand at 10.30 a.m. to go to the market to buy a pair of bullocks. But one of them could not reach the appointed place even after one hour, as there was heavy rain. Should he be blamed? (Yes)	34	48	76
16. Villagers in India are without work for long periods of time. In such a context, would you approve of the introduction of machines like tractors, transport buses, mills for grinding grains. etc.? (Yes)	77	82	71
17. In rural areas, it is not common for labourers to come to work at any fixed time. But in factories, it is necessary that they should report for duty at a fixed time. If they are late by two or three minutes, they are not allowed to work, and lose their wage. Is this a fair practice? (Yes)	68	52	70

Table 5.2 (Continued)

Statements	Azamgarh (N = 200)	Saharanpur (N = 200)	Trichur (N = 200)
18. Some farmers plan their work in advance, while others carry out their work as the necessity arises. Which is the more preferable pattern of work? (Advance planning)	42	76	91
19. You have been cultivating particular crops in your fields for a long time. In such a context, if the agricultural department advises you to switch over to some new agricultural practice (like fish farming), which can double your income, would you change? (Yes)	75	56	79
20. Suppose a factory has been established near your village, giving scope for new activities like opening a tea shop, grocery shop or vegetable shop. In such a context, would you leave your traditional occupation and take up a new occupation? (Yes)	72	59	85
21. Are you doing agriculture (trade) to make money or because your forefathers have been engaged in it? (Make money)	15	38	71
22. Do you agree with the religious teaching that one should not have attachment to material possessions? (No)	6	24	46

Note: Responses indicating modern values are given in brackets.

Items 1 and 2 enquired whether the respondents cherished the value of sharing of income, particularly fortunes, among brothers. Responses to these two items showed the widespread prevalence of this value in all the areas. Those who believed that one need not share his fortune (lottery) with his brothers, but may utilise it for his own needs, formed 23 per cent of the respondents in Azamgarh, 32 per cent in Saharanpur and 48 per cent in Trichur. Those who believed that their brothers working in urban areas need not support them was also relatively small—16 per cent in Azamgarh, 28 per cent in Saharanpur, and 38 per cent in Trichur. These responses reflect the strong fraternal bond prevailing among the respondents.

Item 3 enquired whether the respondents preferred to mobilise the labour required for their agricultural operations through the exchange of labour, or by hiring labourers. In Azamgarh, only 16 per cent of the respondents opted for hiring of labourers, against 53 per cent in Saharanpur, and 71 per cent in Trichur.

Items 4, 5 and 8 enquired about the extent to which the respondents valued the criteria of economic efficiency in the selection of personnel, price in market transactions, and technical knowledge and finances in business partnerships. Responses to Item 4 showed that those who valued efficiency of work as the criterion of selection formed 40 per cent of the respondents from Azamgarh, 45 per cent from Saharanpur and 49 per cent from Trichur. This means that in all the areas, there was a discounting of efficiency and preference for local considerations. Item 5 enquired whether the respondents gave priority to caste or price in an important transaction like the sale of their property. This item showed that 68 per cent of Azamgarh respondents, 69 per cent from Saharanpur and 90 per cent from Trichur gave priority to price over caste in such a transaction. Nevertheless, it is interesting to note that for 31 per cent of the respondents from Azamgarh and 32 per cent from Saharanpur, the caste of the customer is an important criterion in such a transaction. Item 8 enquired about another dimension of the caste and kinship sentiment affecting economic transactions—whether the respondents preferred as a business partner a close relative or one who has the financial capacity and knowledge to carry on the business. Those who preferred one with financial and technical knowledge (performance criteria) formed 60 per cent of the respondents from Azamgarh, 67 per cent from Saharanpur and 87 per cent from Trichur.

Items 6, 7, 9 and 10 enquired about the extent to which prejudices about Harijans were held by the respondents. In the past there were restrictions on Harijans entering village temples and offering worship and on their using transport services, public restaurants, and so on. The responses to these items showed that there has been a considerable weakening of the traditional prejudices. Item 6 showed that 76 per cent of the Azamgarh respondents, 73 per cent from Saharanpur and 95 per cent from Trichur do not believe in restricting Harijans from worshipping at village temples. Item 7 showed that a more or less similar proportion of respondents from the three areas were against the idea of caste-based groups being formed for the celebration of village festivals.

Items 9 and 10 enquired whether the respondents approved the behaviour of Harijans as social equals with members of the higher castes, like Brahmins. Such equality in the relations between persons of different castes envisages their sitting side-by-side in a bus or restaurant. Responses to these items indicate a considerable weakening of the concept of inequality underlying the ideology of caste in all the areas. Those who believed that it is appropriate for a Harijan to sit by the side of a Brahmin in a bus formed 72 per cent of the respondents in Azamgarh, 70 per cent in Saharanpur and 96 per cent in Trichur. Those who believed that it is appropriate for a Brahmin and a Harijan to be served side by side in a village restaurant formed 80 per cent of the respondents in Azamgarh, 70 per cent in Saharanpur and 98 per cent in Trichur.

Items 11 and 13 enquired about the pattern of relations envisaged by those in higher and lower positions. The question in Item 11 is whether agricultural labourers should accept the wage paid to them by farmers or have the right to demand a proper wage. Those who believed that labourers had the right to demand wages form 56 per cent of the respondents in Azamgarh, 71 per cent in Saharanpur and 90 per cent in Trichur. Item 13 shows that those who believed that a clerk need not be respectful to his superior formed 40 per cent, 44 per cent and 19 per cent of the respondents from the three areas, respectively.

Item 12 shows that those who felt it desirable to take away a part of the wealth of the rich and use it for the benefit of the poor formed 66 per cent of the respondents from Azamgarh, 76 per cent from Saharanpur and 91 per cent from Trichur.

Punctuality is an important value and an important requirement of a modern society, while its requirement was less demanding in a traditional society. Responses to Items 14. 15, 16 and 17 reflect respondents' values about punctuality. The percentage of respondents who feel the need to enforce punctuality among children formed 59 per cent in Azamgarh, 52 per cent in Saharanpur, and 74 per cent in Trichur (Item 14). Item 15 enquired whether a person who has fixed an appointment with his friend to visit a market at a fixed time, but cannot keep his promise, should be blamed. It was believed by 34 per cent of the respondents in

Azamgarh, 48 per cent in Saharanpur and 76 per cent in Trichur that such a person should be blamed. Item 17 enquired whether the observance of strict punctuality for factory labour was desirable. It was seen that 68 per cent of the Azamgarh respondents, 52 per cent from Saharanpur and 70 per cent from Trichur felt it necessary. While these responses indicated the general acceptance of the need for punctuality, the degree of its acceptance varied in the three areas. Its acceptance was less in the less developed area, and more in the more developed area.

Item 16 enquired about the attitude of the respondents regarding the use of machines. A vast proportion of the respondents in all the areas had a favourable attitude to the adoption of machines. They constituted 77 per cent in Azamgarh, 82 per cent in Saharanpur and 71 per cent in Trichur.

Item 18 enquired whether the respondents thought it desirable to have advance planning of agricultural and other activities, or whether they preferred to carry them out on an *ad hoc* basis. Those who valued advance planning formed 42 per cent of the respondents in Azamgarh, 76 per cent in Saharanpur and 91 per cent in Trichur.

Items 19 and 20 enquired about the willingness of the respondents to change from their traditional occupations and take up new ones. It was seen that 75 per cent of the Azamgarh respondents, 56 per cent from Saharanpur and 79 per cent from Trichur were willing to change their cropping or occupational pattern and adopt new ones. The same trend was shown by Item 20 as well.

Item 21 enquired whether the respondents practised a particular occupation because it was their traditional occupation, or whether it was the most profitable one in the given situation. Those who followed the occupation on economic consideration formed 15 per cent of the Azamgarh respondents, 38 per cent from Saharanpur and 71 per cent from Trichur.

Item 22 enquired about the extent to which the respondents subscribed to the view that one should not have attachment to material possessions. Only a small proportion of the respondents— 6 per cent in Azamgarh, 24 per cent in Saharanpur and 46 per cent in Trichur—had given up this traditional value, reflecting the widespread belief in the transient nature of the world.

Responses to the 22 items indicated a weakening of traditional ideologies, such as the spirit of caste, the desire for equity, the need for punctuality and the need to follow occupations on the basis of economic rationality, reflecting considerable modernisation in the value orientation of the respondents. However, the respondents strongly believed that one may not have attachment to material possessions, which can seriously weaken the motivation and effort for accumulation of material possessions, a very necessary condition for economic growth.

Responses to the 22 items were scored according to the procedure described earlier. The average scores obtained by the respondents were 11.38 in Azamgarh, 12.6 in Saharanpur and 16.02 in Trichur. The value of F shows that the variations in the mean scores obtained by the respondents were significant at the 1 per cent level: $F (2,597) = 248.9$; $P < 0.01$. The HSD test also showed that the difference in the three mean values was significant at the 1 per cent level. This indicates that the pattern of social values prevailing in Azamgarh, Saharanpur and Trichur varied. Value orientation was more conservative in less developed Azamgarh, and more modern in Saharanpur, and the most modern in Trichur.

Values about Human Relations

Values and norms associated with family, caste and social status play a major role in shaping human relations in a society. To understand the pattern of values about human relations held by the respondents from the three areas, 15 value-loaded statements were put to them. These statements and the percentage of respondents whose responses indicated modern values are given in Table 5.3.

Items 4, 5 and 13 in Table 5.3 deal with husband-wife relations. In a traditional household, the husband is treated as the head, and the wife is given a subordinate position. Item 4 shows that respondents who favour equal status for the husband and wife formed 72 per cent in Azamgarh, 90 per cent in Saharanpur and 75 per cent in Trichur. Item 5 shows that among the Azamgarh respondents, only 47 per cent believed that *sati* was not a desirable custom while 75 per cent of the respondents from Saharanpur and 91 per cent from Trichur were against the practice of *sati*. However, 69 per cent of the Azamgarh respondents approved the remarriage of young widows (Item 6). Compared to this, 89 per cent from

Table 5.3

*Statements Used for Understanding Values about Human Relations and
the Percentage of Respondents with Modern Values*

Statements	Azamgarh (N = 200)	Saharanpur (N = 200)	Trichur (N = 200)
1. Is the character of a person mainly determined by his caste or by his education? (Education)	77	79	97
2. Is obedience and respect for those in authority necessary? (No)	19	40	5
3. Do you think that inter-caste marriages are desirable? (Yes)	66	64	82
4. Do you think that the husband and wife should have equal status? (Yes)	72	90	75
5. Do you think that the old custom of *sati* was a desirable practice? (No)	47	75	91
6. Do you think that a young widow without children should marry again? (Yes)	69	89	97
7. Do you think that a female officer can be as efficient as a male officer? (Yes)	50	80	73
8. Do you think that young persons must be obedient to elders irrespective of their educational differences? (No)	27	22	5
9. The average level of intelligence of Harijans is lower than that of higher castes? (No)	60	56	78
10. The condition of a man's present life is determined by what he has done in his past life? (No)	48	37	72
11. It is due to the exploitation by the rich that some have become poor? (Yes)	61	80	71
12. Do you think that the caste system is a good way of ordering society? (No)	31	63	63
13. If a woman is ill-treated by her husband, should she go in for divorce? (Yes)	65	78	65
14. Is it one's duty to favour members of one's caste? (No)	60	60	93
15. Would it be possible to have a society where wealth is equally distributed? (Yes)	48	61	40

Note: Responses indicating modern values are given in brackets.

Saharanpur and 97 per cent from Trichur approved of widow re-marriage. Item 13 enquired whether the respondents approved of a wife seeking divorce if she was ill-treated by her husband. Those who approved constituted 65 per cent in Azamgarh and Trichur, and 78 per cent in Saharanpur.

Item 7 shows that those who believed that a female officer can be as efficient as a male officer formed 50 per cent of the respondents in Azamgarh, 80 per cent in Saharanpur and 73 per cent in Trichur.

While Item 2 examines respondents'. evaluation of relations between the old and the young, Item 8 examines the qualities expected from those in authority. Younger persons were expected to be obedient to those in authority; those who did not subscribe to this value formed 27 per cent in Azamgarh, 22 per cent in Saharanpur and 5 per cent in Trichur (Item 8). Respondents who believed that those in authority need not be respected were small in all the areas.

Items 1, 9, 12 and 14 enquired about the extent to which the respondents believed in traditional values about caste. Item 1 enquired whether the respondents believed in the traditional value that a person's behaviour was determined by virtue of his birth in a particular caste. A sizeable proportion of the respondents from all the areas were of the opinion that it is education, and not caste, that determines the character of a person. Item 9 enquired about the extent to which the respondents believed that members of lower castes were less intelligent. Those who did not believe this formed 60 per cent in Azamgarh, 56 per cent from Saharanpur and 78 per cent from Trichur. Favouritism to members of one's caste is believed to be a positive value in India, but Item 14 shows that a majority of the respondents in all the areas had given up this value, forming 60 per cent in Azamgarh and Saharanpur, and 93 per cent in Trichur. Item 12 shows that 31 per cent of the respondents from Azamgarh, and 63 per cent from Saharanpur and Trichur believed that the caste system was not a good principle of social stratification. Item 3 shows that respondents who approved of inter-caste marriages formed 66 per cent, 64 per cent and 82 per cent in the three areas.

It is seen from Item 10 that though the majority of the respondents from Azamgarh and Saharanpur believed in *karma*, such a view was not popular in Trichur. On the other hand, those who subscribed to the theory of exploitation as the cause of poverty formed 61 per cent, 80 per cent and 71 per cent in the three areas (Item 11). Those who believed that an egalitarian society can be created by redistributing wealth formed 48 per cent in Azamgarh, 61 per cent in Saharanpur and 40 per cent in Trichur (Item 15).

The mean scores obtained by the respondents on the 15 items were computed, as earlier. They were 8.03 in Azamgarh, 9.66 in Saharanpur and 10.03 in Trichur. The F value indicates that the mean values among the areas differed significantly at the 1 per cent level, showing that belief in modern values is more in Trichur and the least in Azamgarh, with an intermediate status at Saharanpur: $F (2,597) = 74.28$ $P < 0.01$. HSD tests also show that the variations in the average scores obtained by the respondents from Azamgarh and Saharanpur differed significantly at the 1 per cent level. However, the difference in the average scores of the Saharanpur and Trichur respondents were not significant.

Values about Agronomic Practices

To understand the values of the respondents about the adoption of modern methods of agronomic practices, four statements were administered (Table 5.4). Among these, Items 2, 3 and 4 enquired whether the respondents continued to evaluate agricultural inputs (like bone powder and human excreta) on a ritual or rational basis. Item 2 shows that those who were willing to use bone powder, an apparently polluting item, formed 29 per cent in Azamgarh, 35 per cent in Saharanpur and 94 per cent in Trichur. Those who indicated readiness to use human excreta constituted 75 per cent, 62 per cent and 94 per cent in the three areas, respectively. The percentage of respondents who favourably viewed the use of chemical fertilisers constituted 53 per cent in Azamgarh, 55 per cent in Saharanpur and 41 per cent in Trichur (Item 4). Only a few respondents in the three areas cherished the traditional norm that a Brahmin should not wield a plough (Item 1).

The responses to the four items were scored according to the earlier procedure. The mean scores obtained by the respondents from Azamgarh, Saharanpur and Trichur were 2.36, 2.53 and 3.10, respectively. The F value showed that the mean values

Table 5.4
*Statements Used for Understanding the Values about Agronomic Practices
and the Percentage of Respondents with Modern Values*

Statements	Azamgarh (N = 200)	Saharanpur (N = 200)	Trichur (N = 200)
1. It is laid down in the scriptures that Brahmins should never plough a field. Do you approve of this prescription? (No)	82	76	83
2. Agricultural scientists say that bone powder is good manure. Would you spray it yourself in your field? (Yes)	29	35	94
3. Scientists say that human excreta is good manure. Would you be interested in utilising it in your field? (Yes)	75	62	94
4. As chemical fertilisers spoil the quality of the soil, they should not be used extensively? (No)	53	55	41

Note: Responses indicating modern values are given in brackets.

differed significantly at the 1 per cent level: F (2,597) = 23.16, P < 0.01. To find out the inter-group variation between the areas, the HSD test was used, and it showed that the difference in the mean values obtained by the respondents from the three areas was significant at the 1 per cent level.

Values about Livestock Farming

Livestock farming is an important activity in rural areas. It complements crop production though it is sometimes carried out independently. It has various components, like the raising of cattle, buffaloes, goats, pigs and poultry. Although ecological, technological and economic factors should be the main criteria in the raising of various kinds of livestock, social values about different livestock also play an important role in their adoption. Social values give livestock activities different meanings, precluding the adoption of an entirely economic and scientifically rational approach to livestock farming.

To understand the value orientation of the respondents about various livestock activities, their responses were sought on 12 statements regarding their values about various livestock activities. In Table 5.5, the statements used for this purpose and the percentage of respondents whose responses indicated belief in rational values are given.

In India, fishing is considered a polluting occupation, which brings down the status of those who pursue it. In most parts of the country, fishermen are untouchables, occupying low social status. It is in such a context that questions 1, 2 and 3 were posed to the respondents. Item 3 shows that those who believed that fish farming is not a polluting occupation formed 67 per cent of the respondents in Azamgarh, 69 per cent in Saharanpur and 91 per cent in Trichur. Item 1 shows that 78 per cent of the respondents in Azamgarh and Saharanpur, and 95 per cent in Trichur did not believe that only members of the fisherman caste can succeed in pisciculture. This is an indication of the widespread prevalence of the value that any person belonging to any caste can follow any occupation. Responses to Item 2 show that those who believed that their social status would be adversely affected if they took up pisciculture formed more than two-thirds of the respondents in Azamgarh and Saharanpur, and half of the respondents from Trichur. Those who believed that pisciculture should be encouraged formed 60 per cent of the respondents from Azamgarh, 70 per cent from Saharanpur and 96 per cent from Trichur. These responses indicate, at least at the verbal level, a favourable attitude to piscicultural activities, which is considered to be a polluting occupation.

Cattle being the main component of livestock production in rural areas, a variety of secular and non-secular values are associated with them, making these animals more than a source of income. Items 5 to 10 try to understand the nature of the values held by the respondents regarding the rearing of cattle and related practices. It is generally believed by experts that the excessive number of cattle, which cannot be fed properly, should be culled. However, Item 7 shows that only a few (11 per cent) of the Azamgarh respondents, and 39 per cent of the Saharanpur respondents, held such a view. For the majority of the people in these areas, a cow is still more than an economic asset. Only in Trichur is the culling of useless animals accepted. The usual reason given by villagers for having a reverential attitude to cattle is that people

Table 5.5
*Statements Used for Understanding Values about Livestock Practices
and the Percentage of Respondents with Modern Values*

Statements	Azamgarh (N = 200)	Saharanpur (N = 200)	Trichur (N = 200)
1. Would a person not belonging to the fisherman caste succeed if he takes up fish farming? (Yes)	78	78	95
2. Do you think that it is below the dignity of a person of good social standing to take up fish farming? (Yes)	63	61	48
3. Do you think that fish farming is a polluting occupation? (No)	67	69	91
4. Do you think that as Indians are mainly vegetarian, fish farming should not be encouraged in India? (No)	60	70	96
5. Do you think that artificially inseminating a cow is a sin? (No)	81	76	84
6. Do you think that a cow should be milked only after the calf drinks milk to its full satisfaction? (No)	65	69	77
7. Do you think that like weeds are removed from farms, useless cows should be killed? (Yes)	11	39	85
8. Since we grow by drinking the milk of cows, we should be reverential to the cow as we are reverential to our mothers? (No)	26	31	73
9. It is better to have fewer cows giving higher yields than a large number of cows with lower yields. (Yes)	69	83	90
10. A cow is an auspicious animal. (No)	49	53	88
11. Do you think that a respectable man would raise pigs to make money? (Yes)	18	50	78
12. Is poultry farming an honourable occupation? (Yes)	46	57	91

Note: Responses indicating modern values are given in brackets.

grow by drinking its milk. Therefore, one should respect a cow as one respects one's mother. Responses to Item 8 show that such an attitude was widely held in Azamgarh and Saharanpur. Those who did not hold such a value formed 26 per cent in Azamgarh, and 31 per cent in Saharanpur. But, in Trichur, 73 per cent of the respondents held a modern value in this respect. Item 10 is also a related question and enquired whether the respondents believed that a cow is an auspicious animal. According to the belief of the villagers, there are 'auspecious' things, animals and persons, whose presence would make a positive contribution to one's well-being. Therefore, such things are to be preserved and looked after well. The response to Item 10 indicates the widespread belief in Azamgarh and Saharanpur that a cow is an auspicious animal. Responses to Items 7, 8 and 10 indicate that a rational attitude towards cows prevailed only among the Trichur respondents. The reverential attitude towards cows prevailing in Azamgarh and Saharanpur can be a hindrance to dairy development in these areas. However, Item 9 reflects the belief widely held by the respondents in all the areas that it is better to have fewer cows with better yields than a larger number with less yields.

Item 5 shows that respondents were not against the artificial insemination of cows. Item 6 shows that those who believed that a cow should be milked only after the calf has drunk milk to its satisfaction, were only a few.

Items 11 and 12 enquired about the attitude of the respondents regarding piggery and poultry farming. Pork is an important component of the diet of the people in developed countries, making hogging an important livestock activity. But responses to Item 11 showed the deeply held view, particularly in Azamgarh, that raising pigs, let alone eating pork, was not a respectable activity. Such a view was held by 82 per cent of the Azamgarh respondents and 50 per cent of the respondents from Saharanpur. Compared to this, in Trichur, most (78 per cent) of the respondents did not believe that hogging was a degrading activity.

Poultry is another important livestock activity in developed countries, and in a few places in India. It is an activity which can make a significant contribution to the economic condition of the farmers. Item 12 enquired about the value orientation of the respondents about poultry farming. Those respondents who favoured poultry farming formed 46 per cent in Azamgarh, 57 per cent in Saharanpur and 91 per cent in Trichur.

Evaluation of economic activities according to economic rationality, potential profit and income, is an important requirement for the full utilisation of resources, facilitating economic development. When occupations are evaluated on non-economic criteria, like purity and pollution, economic rationality becomes subordinated to such values. Piggery and poultry are believed to be degrading occupations, according to the values of a large proportion of the population. Such a value orientation limited the scope for the development of livestock activities based on them. Similarly, the culling of cattle is necessary for better returns from good animals. But responses to various items showed that in the value orientation of the respondents from Azamgarh and Saharanpur, the main criterion for evaluating livestock activities was not economic rationality, but considerations of ritual purity. Such an orientation limited the scope for the full utilisation of the livestock potential available in these areas.

The responses to the 12 items in Table 5.5 were scored as earlier. The mean scores obtained by the respondents were 6.30 in Azamgarh, 7.37 in Saharanpur and 9.88 in Trichur. The F ratio showed that the variation in the mean values of the respondents from the three areas were significant at the 1 per cent level: $F(2,597) = 255.84$ $P < 0.01$. Tukey's HSD test also showed that the variations in the mean values were significant at the 1 per cent level.

· *Values about Nutrition and Health*

Food is consumed primarily for nutrition, and rationality requires its evaluation on the basis of nutritive and health criteria. However, in many societies there are various other considerations, with reference to which dietary items are evaluated, making scientific ideas about food items subordinate to such values.

For understanding the values held by the respondents from the three areas about dietary and health matters, their responses were sought on 9 items given in Table 5.6. Among these, the first three enquired about the basic values guiding the choice of dietary items. Item 1 shows that those who gave priority to nutrition formed 67 per cent of the respondents from Azamgarh, 82 per cent from Saharanpur and 67 per cent from Trichur. However, responses to Item 2 show that even in a difficult situation, a majority

Table 5.6
Statements Used for Understanding Values about Nutrition and Health
and the Percentage of Respondents with Modern Values

Statements	Azamgarh (N = 200)	Saharanpur (N = 200)	Trichur (N = 200)
1. In selecting food, to what do you give more importance—taste or nutrition? (Nutrition)	67	82	67
2. Do you think that even if one has to go without food, one should not eat food items which are ritually impure? (No)	42	42	55
3. Most of the religions have prohibited eating certain items (e.g., beef by Hinduism; pork by Islam). Do you think that one should follow such teachings? (No)	20	30	61
4. Do you think that whatever care one takes about one's health, one will still die of a predestined cause? (No)	46	41	36
5. Do you think that whatever care one may take, one will still die at the predestined time? (No)	42	36	37
6. Do you think that persons born under certain stars (period of time) are likely to get particular diseases? (No)	33	59	51
7. Some people say that God (goddess) will be unhappy if we vaccinate our child against smallpox. Do you think so? (No)	46	79	71
8. Do you think that it is better to depend on God than on doctors for our health? (No)	48	68	86
9. Some people say that snake bites can be cured by accurately chanting *mantras*. Do you believe this is true? (No)	53	63	96

Note: Responses indicating modern values are given in brackets.

of the respondents would evaluate dietary items on ritual criteria and would forego food items which were not ritually pure. Those who were not bothered about the ritual quality of the food formed 42 per cent in Azamgarh and Saharanpur, and 55 per cent in

Trichur. This implies that ritual purity is a very important criterion in the choice of food. Item 3 also raises a similar issue, and responses to it showed that both in Azamgarh (80 per cent) and Saharanpur (70 per cent), respondents strongly believed in the need to observe religious taboos on food. However, in Trichur, 61 per cent of the respondents were not concerned with such taboos.

Items 4, 5 and 6 enquired about the fatalistic beliefs of the respondents. Fatalistic beliefs (such as, whatever care one may take about one's health, one is bound to die of a predestined cause and at a predestined time) are widespread in rural areas. Responses to Items 4 and 5 indicated the strong belief held in all the areas in this matter. Those who did not believe in the predestined cause of death formed 46 per cent in Azamgarh, 41 per cent in Saharanpur and 36 per cent in Trichur, and those who did not believe in the predestined time of death formed 42 per cent, 36 per cent and 37 per cent in the three areas, respectively. Nevertheless, there was widespread acceptance of the role of doctors in the maintenance of health, forming 48 per cent of the respondents in Azamgarh, 68 per cent in Saharanpur and 86 per cent in Trichur (Item 8).

Item 6 reflects the widespread belief that the time of birth of a person influences his prosperity. Those who did not hold such a belief formed 33 per cent in Azamgarh, 59 per cent in Saharanpur and 51 per cent in Trichur.

Items 7 and 9 enquired about the prevalence of some superstitious beliefs among the respondents. One such belief prevalent in many parts of the country is that snake bite can be cured by the accurate chanting of mantras (Item 9). Those who did not hold such a belief formed 53 per cent in Azamgarh, 63 per cent in Saharanpur and 96 per cent in Trichur. The superstition that vaccination against smallpox could kindle the wrath of the goddess was rejected by 46 per cent of the respondents of Azamgarh, 79 per cent from Saharanpur and 71 per cent from Trichur.

Responses to the 9 items were scored as described earlier. The mean scores obtained by the respondents on the 9 items were 3.95 in Azamgarh, 5.01 in Saharanpur and 5.71 in Trichur. The F ratio showed that the variations in the mean scores were significant at the 1 per cent level: $F_{(2,597)} = 57.73$ $P < 0.01$. The HSD test also confirmed that the variations in the mean scores were significant at the 1 per cent level.

Values about Fertility Control

Values about the number of children desired by a person, the use of fertility control practices, and so on, influence fertility behaviour. To understand the pattern of values held by the respondents about fertility control and various practices associated with it, their responses were sought on 13 different items, which are given in Table 5.7. Among these, Items 1 and 12 show that in all the areas, the idea that 'children are God's blessing' and that 'God will take care of all persons for whom He has given life,' have considerably weakened, and a majority of the respondents accept the need for fertility control. Those who recognise the need for fertility control formed 52 per cent in Azamgarh, 70 per cent in Saharanpur and 78 per cent in Trichur (Item 1). Item 12 also shows a similar trend. Item 6 shows the widespread opinion of the respondents in the three areas (72 per cent in Azamgarh, 83 per cent in Saharanpur and 90 per cent in Trichur) that information about birth conrol should be taught to everyone in the society.

One point usually stressed by the opponents of the family planning programme is that self-restraint is sufficient for fertility control and there is no need to popularise various birth control techniques and practices. Item 2 shows that 40 per cent of the respondents in Azamgarh, 70 per cent in Saharanpur and 50 per cent in Trichur believed that self-restraint alone would not be sufficient for controlling fertility.

Item 9 enquired whether the respondents felt that the increasing pressure of population was affecting the prosperity of the country. Those who believed that if there are less people in the country, the level of living would be higher formed 30 per cent in Azamgarh, 40 per cent in Saharanpur and 79 per cent in Trichur. Responses to Item 10 show that the majority of the respondents from Azamgarh and Saharanpur did not consider their children to be a source of income.

Items 3, 7 and 8 enquired whether the respondents believed that birth control measures were morally objectionable practices. It is seen from Item 3 that 66 per cent of the respondents from Azamgarh, 71 per cent from Saharanpur and 87 per cent from Trichur do not consider it a sin to adopt fertility control practices. Item 7 raises a related question, namely, whether the respondents believed

Table 5.7
*Statements Used for Understanding Values about the Control of Fertility
and the Percentage of Respondents with Modern Values*

Statements	Azamgarh (N = 200)	Saharanpur (N = 200)	Trichur (N = 200)
1. Do you think that children are God's blessings, and man should not try to interfere with their birth? (No)	52	70	78
2. Do you think that encouragement of moral restraint would be sufficient for birth control, and there is no need for any family planning programme? (No)	40	70	50
3. Do you consider it a sin to practise birth control? (No)	66	71	87
4. Do you think that a respectable · person would adopt family planning measures? (Yes)	46	45	89
5. Do you think that if a man undergoes a vasectomy operation, he will become impotent? (No)	53	57	68
6. Do you think that information about birth control should be taught to everybody in society? (Yes)	72	83	90
7. Do you think that easy availability of contraceptives will lead to an increase in immorality? (No)	26	55	66
8. Do you think that it is a sin to have an abortion? (No)	38	55	56
9. Do you think that if there were less people in our country, we would have been more comfortable? (Yes)	30	40	79
10. Do you think that if there are a large number of children, there would be a larger income for the household? (No)	68	66	41
11. Do you think that a vasectomy would would make a man unfit for hard work? (No)	32	55	72
12. Do you think that God will take care of all persons for whom He has given life and we need not bother about birth control? (No)	55	63	86
13. Do you think that if there are fewer children in a household, they can be better educated? (Yes)	86	87	99

Note: Responses indicating modern values are given in brackets.

that the easy availability of contraceptives would lead to an increase in promiscuity. Such a view was widely held in Azamgarh, where only 26 per cent of the respondents did not have such apprehensions. But in Saharanpur and Trichur, 55 per cent and 66 per cent of the respondents, respectively, did not hold such view. Item 8 enquired whether the respondents considered it a sin to resort to abortion. Responses to this item also show that only in Azamgarh did a large percentage of the respondents hold such a view. Those who accepted it formed 38 per cent in Azamgarh, 55 per cent in Saharanpur and 56 per cent in Trichur.

Items 5 and 11 show that prejudices against vasectomy (for instance, that it leads to sexual impotency and incapacitates one from hard work) have weakened. Item 4 shows that notwithstanding such a general acceptance of birth control measures, there was a certain amount of ambiguity about the acceptance of fertility control measures among the respondents from Azamgarh and Saharanpur. Those who perceived it as a respectable practice constituted 46 per cent in Azamgarh and 45 per cent in Saharanpur, as against 89 per cent in Trichur. Thus, value orientation more favourable to the adoption of fertility control measures prevailed in Trichur.

Responses to the 13 items in Table 5.7 were scored as earlier, and the mean scores obtained by the respondents were 6.60 in Azamgarh, 8.21 in Saharanpur and 9.51 in Trichur. The F ratio showed that the variations in the mean scores obtained by the respondents from the three areas were statistically significant at the 1 per cent level: $F(2,597) = 116.7$; $P < 0.01$. Tukey's HSD test also showed that the variations in the mean scores among the respondents from the three areas were significant at the 1 per cent level.

Values about Commercial Activities

Commerce is an important component of a modern economy and society. But in an underdeveloped society, households and villages are mostly self-sufficient. In such societies, the extra requirements of individual households are mostly met through goods and services received on the basis of reciprocity, gifts, patron-client relations, and so on. For example, it is still customary in villages to mobilise the required goods and services for celebrating a marriage in a household on the basis of reciprocity. But with development, such mobilisation is replaced with commerce. For example, when a feast has to be given in a city to celebrate a marriage, it is arranged by a catering contractor. It is seldom that relatives and caste-men undertake the preparation of food, or serving it. Marketing activities are likely to be smooth if the values related to marketing activities are in harmony with the requirements of marketing. Values emphasising affective neutrality about customers, specificity in relations, universalism, lack of distrust of strangers, economic rationality, and so on, favour commercial activities.

To understand the values about commercial activities held by the respondents, their responses were sought on 14 statements. These statements and the percentage of respondents with modern rational values about commercial activities are given in Table 5.8. Among these, Items 1 and 2 enquired about the values of the respondents regarding economic goods and services. As was seen earlier, the villagers would often value their cattle and other economic goods on considerations other than their mere economic utility. For example, as enquired in Item 1, peasants kept their animals like buffaloes even after they became unproductive. It is seen from this that those who believed that a buffalo may be disposed of after it ceased to be useful formed 67 per cent of the respondents in Azamgarh, 57 per cent in Saharanpur and 91 per cent in Trichur. Item 2 shows that a majority of the respondents in all the areas preferred the labour-farmer relation to be a diffused, life-long, relation rather than a specific one.

Item 4 enquired whether the respondents believed that any person can be trained to perform the professions followed by members of another caste, for example, whether a Harijan can be trained to become a barber. Responses to this item showed that 42 per cent of the respondents from Azamgarh, 59 per cent from Saharanpur and 49 per cent from Trichur believed that, through training, one can be equipped to do any job. Item 3 shows that respondents who are not bothered about the caste background of a tea-shop owner formed 47 per cent in Azamgarh, 56 per cent in Saharanpur and 92 per cent in Trichur.

Item 13 enquired whether the respondents would like their daughters to be trained as nurses, serving persons belonging to different castes. It is seen that 63 per cent of the Azamgarh respondents, 79 per cent from Saharanpur and 94 per cent from Trichur were interested in doing so.

Honesty in one's dealings with others and a sense of trust of

Table 5.8
*Statements Used for Understanding Commercial Values and
the Percentage of Respondents with Modern Values*

Statements	Azamgarh (N = 200)	Saharanpur (N = 200)	Trichur (N = 200)
1. Would you sell a buffalo when it becomes old? (Yes)	67	57	91
2. Do you think that after a labourer has become old and weak, the farmer should continue to employ him, as he has no other source of living? (No)	49	42	20
3. One should not take tea/food from a tea shop maintained by a Harijan? (No)	47	56	92
4. Even if a Harijan is trained to become a barber, he would not become a good barber. (No)	42	59	49
5. Even though a shop owner may claim to make sweets in 'pure *ghee*,' it may not be true. (No)	60	54	15
6. One cannot expect to get 'pure' food from a restaurant. (No)	47	54	9
7. If one wants to drink pure milk, one has to keep a cow or buffalo. (No)	14	35	5
8. If one buys goods from an unknown trader, there is the possibility of one being cheated. (No)	13	40	13
9. Do you think that it is better to make payment for the services of a barber, washerman, etc., in grain rather than cash? (No)	69	48	99
10. As far as possible, one should try to produce all one's requirements, instead of buying them. (No)	15	43	10
11. Do you think that villagers should only buy things which are produced in their own villages? (No)	43	49	80
12. Some clever farmers sometimes do not properly separate the chaff from the grain and sell it as good grain. Is this a fair practice? (No)	84	79	93
13. Would you like your daughter to be trained as a nurse where she has to serve patients belonging to different castes? (Yes)	63	79	94

Table 5.8 (Continued)

Items	Azamgarh (N = 200)	Saharanpur (N = 200)	Trichur (N = 200)
14. Who will succeed in business: a trader who sells things of good quality or one who performs *pooja* daily but sells inferior things? (Good quality)	86	90	99

Note: Responses indicating modern values are given in brackets.

strangers are basic requirements for the development of commercial activities. The two are closely linked. As one prepares goods and services for sale, one's customers become strangers, breaking the particularistic relationship constituted through kinship, caste, village, and so on. When one's customers become members of an 'outgroup', there is the basic question of whether one should be honest to such strangers. Item 12 enquired about this aspect, and showed the widespread disapproval of deliberately not separating the chaff from the grain and selling it as good grain. Item 14 is a related question, and responses to it reflect the widespread belief in the need for honesty in commercial transactions, which was believed by 86 per cent of the Azamgarh respondents, 90 per cent from Saharanpur and 99 per cent from Trichur.

The other side of one's commitment to honesty is one's own perception of other's behaviour on such issues. Item 8 reflected the widespread distrust of strangers prevailing in all the three areas.

Items 5, 6 and 7 enquired about the perception of the respondents regarding traders: whether a trader can be trusted on his word. Item 5 showed that those who believed the claim of a trader to make sweets in pure *ghee* formed 60 per cent of the Azamgarh respondents, 54 per cent in Saharanpur and 15 per cent in Trichur. Those who believed that one can get pure food from a restaurant formed 47 per cent, 54 per cent and 9 per cent in the three areas respectively (Item 6). However, Item 7 showed that those who believed that one can get 'pure milk' from a cowherd formed a small proportion in all the areas—14 per cent in Azamgarh, 35 per cent in Saharanpur and 5 per cent in Trichur.

In Indian village society, the services of the barber, washerman, and so on, are obtained on the basis of patron-client relations rather than trade. Such services are generally not paid for in cash but in kind at the time of harvesting agricultural produce. Item 9 enquired about the preference of the respondents in this matter by enquiring whether the respondents preferred to make payments for these services in kind or cash. Those who preferred to make cash payments for these services formed 69 per cent in Azamgarh, 48 per cent in Saharanpur and 99 per cent in Trichur.

Item 10 enquired about the extent to which respondents believed in the need to practise self-sufficiency in their requirements. Those who believed that individuals need not produce all their requirements formed 15 per cent in Azamgarh, 43 per cent in Saharanpur and 10 per cent in Trichur. Item 11 showed that those who believed that villagers need not produce all their requirements, but may buy them, formed 43 per cent, 49 per cent and 80 per cent, respectively.

Responses to the 14 items were scored according to the procedure described earlier. The average scores obtained by the respondents were 6.96 from Azamgarh, 7.85 from Saharanpur and 7.60 from Trichur. The F ratio showed that the variations in the mean scores obtained by the respondents from the three areas were significant at the 1 per cent level: F (2,597) = 14.21 P < 0.01. However, the HSD test showed that the variations in the mean values between Saharanpur and Trichur were not significant, but that between Azamgarh on the one hand, and Saharanpur and Trichur, on the other, were significant at the 1 per cent level. This shows that while respondents from the less developed area have values less congenial for the development of commercial activities, those from the developed areas have values more congenial for commercial activities.

Self-Assessment

In order to evaluate the self-assessment of respondents, three questions were posed to elicit information on how the respondents rate the level of progress in their life. The level of progress was measured in terms of a ladder with eleven rungs. It was explained to the respondents that each step on the ladder represented different levels of progress in their life. They were asked to rate on which step they were standing currently, on which step they stood five years ago, and on which step they expected to stand after five years. In response to the question of where they were currently standing on the ladder, 4 per cent, 5 per cent and 8 per cent of respondents from Azamgarh, Saharanpur and Trichur respectively rated their present position on the lowest rung of the ladder. Respondents who assessed their current position between the first and fifth steps formed 93 per cent in Azamgarh, 86 per cent in Saharanpur and 91 per cent in Trichur. Very few respondents rated their present position above the fifth rung in all the three blocks and nobody claimed to have reached on the top of the ladder from any of the blocks. This means that most of the respondents felt that they still have to achieve many things in life.

In response to the query of where they stood five years ago, 35 per cent, 22 per cent and 18 per cent of the respondents respectively from Azamgarh, Saharanpur and Trichur said that they were on the lowest rung of the ladder. Those respondents who felt that they stood between the first and fifth rung of the ladder formed 60 per cent of the Azamgarh respondents, 75 per cent from Saharanpur and 79 per cent from Trichur. Those who rated their position above the fifth rung were very low in all the three blocks.

The third question sought to understand the perception of the respondents about their status in the next five years. Those respondents who felt that their position would be on the lowest rung of the ladder formed 1 per cent in Azamgarh, 4 per cent in Saharanpur and 5 per cent in Trichur. Those who believed that their position would be between the first and the fifth rung of the ladder constituted 64 per cent in Azamgarh, 83 per cent in Saharanpur and 83 per cent in Trichur. It was found earlier that very few respondents from all the blocks rated their current position, and their position five years ago, above the sixth step of the ladder. However, 35 per cent of the respondents from Azamgarh, 39 per cent from Saharanpur and 12 per cent from Trichur were optimistic that in the next five years their position would improve.

The responses to each question were placed on a 11-point scale ranging from 0 to 10. The minimum score was 0 and the maximum score was 30. The mean scores obtained by the respondents were 8.97 from Azamgarh, 10.18 from Saharanpur and 8.76 from Trichur. The F value showed that the variation in the mean values among the three areas differed significantly at the 1 per cent level:

F (2.597) = 19.34; P < 0.01. The HSD test showed that the variations in the mean values between Azamgarh and Trichur were not significant but those between Azamgarh and Saharanpur were significant.

Aspirations for Socio-Economic Advancement

To understand the level of aspiration of the respondents for socio-economic advancement, their level of aspiration on five aspects of life were enquired: their aspiration for the level of education for their sons and daughters, their level of income, the type of house they would like to possess, and the amount of wealth they would like to have. Aspiration about these items were enquired at five levels. In Table 5.9, the percentage of respondents having different levels of aspiration on these five items are given. Responses to the five items were scored by giving scores on six-point scales ranging from 0–5. The total score for each respondent against all the 5 items was computed. The mean scores obtained by the respondents of Azamgarh, Saharanpur and Trichur were 13.38, 17.50 and 15.09 respectively. Respondents from Saharanpur obtained the maximum mean value followed by those from Trichur. Computation of the F value showed that the mean values among the areas differed significantly at the 1 per cent level: F (2,597) = 147.74 P < 0.01. In order to find out the inter-group variation between the areas, the HSD test was used. The test showed that variations in the mean values obtained by the respondents from the three areas were significant at the 1 per cent level.

Summary

In this chapter, basic values, values about human relations, agronomic practices, livestock farming, nutrition and health, fertility control, commercial activities, aspiration and self-assessment of the respondents from areas varying in socio-economic development were examined. Respondents from all the areas emphasised the realisation of salvation of the soul, conformity to traditional practices and fatalism. The stress on traditional values was found to be more in Azamgarh, and the least in Trichur. Examination of the social values of the respondents indicated that the sense of

Table 5.9
Percentage of Respondents with Different Levels of Aspiration for
Socio-Economic Advancement

Aspect of Life	Azamgarh (N = 200)	Saharanpur (N = 200)	Trichur (N = 200)
1. All of us want to provide education to our children. How much education you want to give to your son?			
0. None	9	2	1
1. Primary	5	2	1
2. Middle school	13	7	0
3. High school	9	14	21
4. College	17	22	52
5. Medical/engineering/post-graduate	49	54	26
2. How much education you want to give to your daughter?			
0. None	20	6	1
1. Primary	21	19	0
2. Middle school	14	13	0
3. High school	5	8	25
4. College	15	10	51
5. Medical/engineering/post-graduate	27	45	24
3. How much income you would like to have in a month (Rs)?			
0. None	2	1	2
1. Less than 500	22	4	7
2. 500–1,000	42	30	58
3. 1,001–1,500	7	10	30
4. 1,501–2,500	7	12	3
5. 2,501+	22	45	1
4. What type of house you would like to build for yourself?			
0. None	3	2	10
1. Hut with mud wall and thatch	5	2	1
2. House with mud wall and tile roof	21	0	6
3. Small house with brick wall and tile roof	36	15	21
4. House with 4–5 rooms	24	47	52
5. Bungalow	13	36	13
5. How much wealth would you like to possess (Rs)?			
0. None	20	20	20
1. Up to 1 lakh	62	29	25
2. 1–3 lakh	4	11	42
3. 3–6 lakh	2	5	14
4. 6–10 lakh	2	16	1
5. 10 lakh and more	12	20	0

equity, commitment to punctuality, economic rationality in the choice of occupations and aspiration for material possessions were more in Trichur and Saharanpur than in Azamgarh. Rationalisation of an economic activity is essential for income generation and the full use of resources. However, in Azamgarh and Saharanpur livestock activities (like pisciculture and hogging) were evaluated on non-economic criteria, subordinating economic rationality. The same trend was reflected in the pattern of values about nutrition and health practices held by the respondents. Values about the adoption of fertility control measures also showed a similar trend, with respondents from Trichur having the values most favourable to fertility control measures. The value orientation of the respondents from Azamgarh was less congenial for the development of commercial activities, with emphasis on the self-sufficiency of households and villages, and distrust of strangers. In contrast to this, the type of values held by respondents from Saharanpur and Trichur were more congenial for commercial activities. Thus, the pattern of value orientation in areas varying in levels of socio-economic development varied. Values stressing the rational pursuit of economic activities, universalism, specificity in relations, performance and material orientation were the most extensive in the developed area of Trichur, and the least prevalent in the underdeveloped area of Azamgarh. Thus, a close association exists between the level of socio-economic development of an area and the pattern of values prevailing in the area.

6

Correlates of Empirical Knowledge

In Chapters 4 and 5, the salient characteristics of the cognitive and evaluative patterns of culture were examined. It was seen that the cognitive and evaluative patterns varied in areas with different levels of development. In this chapter, an attempt is made to study the variables related to the variations in the empirical knowledge of the respondents. It will also give an estimate of the relative contribution of different independent factors to the variation in knowledge.

The analyses to establish the relationship between the variations in knowledge and the factors related to it are done at different levels. First, the analysis is done at the aggregate level, where the responses to the nine components of cognitive orientation discussed in Chapter 4 are jointly taken into account and treated as the dependent variable by developing an aggregate index of knowledge. As was mentioned earlier, a response indicating knowledge about an item was given a score of 1, and a response indicating lack of knowledge about an item was given a score of 0. The nine components of cognitive orientation together contained 95 items, making it possible for a respondent to have an aggregate score varying between 0 and 95 on the aggregate index of knowledge. Secondly, analysis has been done at the level of each component of cognitive orientation, treating the total scores obtained by a respondent on each component as a dependent variable. Analysis has been done further by aggregating the sample from the three areas into a single group, and treating 600 respondents as a single group, as also by disaggregating the sample based on area into three groups. While the level of knowledge of the respondents as reflected by the scores obtained by them was the dependent variable, the independent variables assumed to influence the level of knowledge were: education of the respondents; their fathers' education; membership in formal associations; exposure to mass media; spatial mobility; types of tools used; value of inputs used; and per capita household income. Details of the method of development of these items are given in Chapter 1.

Linear Multiple Regression Analysis

The analyses to examine the variables associated with the variation in cognitive orientation are done through multiple regression analysis. Regression analysis postulates a causal relationship between a dependent and one or more independent variables. In this analysis, it is assumed that a dependent variable is a linear function of independent variables. Therefore, through regression analysis, it is possible to estimate how much variation in the level of knowledge is explained by the independent variables, jointly and separately. For the purpose of interpreting the data, the value of multiple R (R^2), the relative contribution of independent variables and regression coefficients were derived through the regression analysis. An important measure for the determination of the fitness of regression is R^2. It (R^2) gives the percentage of variance explained by the regression. It is a measure of how much effect a given change in the independent variable has on the dependent variable. The R^2 value gives the total variance explained by a set of independent variables taken together. The individual contribution of each independent variable towards the total explained variance is an index of the relative importance of each variable.

Correlates of Knowledge

In Table 6.1, the results of regression between the aggregate index of knowledge and the eight independent variables are given. These regressions have been computed for the aggregate sample of 600 respondents, and separately for the sample of respondents from Azamgarh, Saharanpur and Trichur. While the regression coefficients indicate the strength of the relation between each independent

Table 6.1
*Results of Multiple Regression Analysis between Aggregate Index of
Knowledge Score and Socio-Economic Characteristics*

Characteristics	Azamgarh (N = 200)	Saharanpur (N = 200)	Trichur (N = 200)	Aggregate (N = 600)
1	2	3	4	5
1. Father's education	1.930	2.454*	−0.010	2.637†
	(3.63)	(5:02)	(0.01)	(5.84)
2. Education of self	0.883	2.547†	8.494†	3.266†
	(2.58)	(10.50)	(24.70)	(10.72)
3. Membership in associations	1.708†	0.174	1.281*	1.359†
	(4.91)	(0.47)	(2.42)	(4.00)
4. Exposure to mass media	0.738†	1.511†	1.215†	1.604†
	(9.87)	(28.69)	(12.57)	(29.39)
5. Spatial mobility	0.389†	0.150	−0.019	0.116
	(4.98)	(2.36)	(0.16)	(1.22)
6. Types of tools used	0.240	0.966	−0.500	−1.869†
	(0.40)	(1.12)	(0.21)	(1.11)
7. Value of inputs used	0.003	−0.001	0.001	0.002†
	(3.02)	(0.65)	(1.71)	(1.75)
8. Per capita monthly income	−0.004	0.003	0.002	0.002
	(0.24)	(0.80)	(0.51)	(0.37)
	$R^2 = 0.291$	$R^2 = 0.483$	$R^2 = 0.415$	$R^2 = 0.544$
	F = 9.8†	F = 22.31†	F = 16.94†	F = 88.14†

Note: Figures in brackets indicate percentage of variance explained by an independent variable.
† = $P < 0.01$; * = $P < 0.05$.

variable and the dependent variable, the F value indicates whether the variation among the independent variables in explaining the dependent variable is significant. As mentioned earlier, R^2 indicates the variation explained by the independent variables together. The values in brackets indicate the relative contribution of each independent variable to the total variation in the contribution of the dependent variable.

In column 5, the regression coefficients R^2 and F ratio for the combined sample (N = 600) are given. The R^2 value of the regression is 0.544, indicating that the independent variables have jointly explained 54.4 per cent of the variation in the level of knowledge. The values of regression coefficients indicate that among the eight independent variables, respondent's education, father's education, membership in formal organisations, level of exposure to mass media, type of tools used, and value of inputs used are related significantly with variation in the level of knowledge. The types of tools used showed a negative association with the level of knowledge. However, the per capita household income of the respondents, and their spatial mobility, are not significantly related with the variation in the level of knowledge of the respondents.

Among the six variables significantly related to variation in the level of knowledge, the most important one was variation in the level of exposure to mass media, which contributed 29.39 per cent to the total variance. The main components of 'mass media exposure' are frequency of visiting towns, cinemas, reading newspapers and listening to the radio. It is interesting to note that mass media is a very powerful source of disseminating knowledge. The second important variable which contributes 10.72 per cent to the variation in knowledge is the level of education of the respondents. Education of the respondents' fathers is also a significant factor, which contributes 5.84 per cent to the total variation in the level of knowledge. Membership in associations is also an important variable, contributing 4.00 per cent to the variation. Among the three economic variables examined, the value of inputs showed a positive association with the variation in the level of knowledge. It is in the expected direction, as those with a higher level of knowledge can be expected to use larger quantities of inputs. While the per capita income of respondents was not significantly related with variation in knowledge, the types of tools used in agricultural production showed a negative relation.

Azamgarh: In column 2, the results of the regression in the case of respondents from Azamgarh is given. Among the eight independent variables, membership of the respondents in associations, their exposure to mass media and spatial mobility are related with the variation in the level of knowledge at the 1 per cent level of significance. R^2 of 0.291 indicates that the eight variables together explain only 29.1 per cent of the total variation in knowledge. As in the case of the aggregate respondents, the variation which contributed the most to the variation in knowledge of the Azamgarh respondents is also exposure to mass media—it contributed 9.87 per cent to the total variation in the level of knowledge. This is followed by spatial mobility contributing 4.98 per cent, and membership in associations contributing 4.91 per cent. Some of the other variables which made small contributions to total variation in knowledge are father's education (3.63 per cent), education of self (2.58 per cent), and value of inputs (3.02 per cent).

Saharanpur: In the case of the Saharanpur respondents (column 3), R^2 of 0.483 indicates that the eight independent variables together explained 48.3 per cent of the variation in the level of knowledge. Among the eight variables, level of education of self and father, and exposure to mass media are significantly related with variation in knowledge. Among these, exposure to mass media explained as much as 28.69 per cent of the variation, followed by education contributing 10.50 per cent. In the case of the Azamgarh respondents, the relative contribution of education to increase in the level of knowledge is very low (2.58 per cent). This is quite understandable, as Azamgarh is a pre-literate society, where education cannot make an important contribution to increase in knowledge. But with the spread of education, as in Saharanpur, education has become an important source for the spread of knowledge in the community. Father's education contributed 5.02 per cent of the variation in the level of knowledge, and spatial mobility 2.36 per cent.

Trichur: In the case of the Trichur respondents (column 4), the R^2 value of 0.415 indicates that 41.5 per cent of the variation in knowledge is explained by the eight variables. Among these, education of the self, exposure to mass media and membership in formal associations are significantly related with variation in the level of knowledge, respectively contributing 24.70 per cent, 12.57 per cent and 2.42 per cent to the variation in knowledge.

The foregoing examination indicates that the main variables which contribute to variation in knowledge are respondents' exposure to mass media and education. Membership in associations and father's education also have significant contributions to it. However, as the eight independent variables together do not explain more than a portion of the variation in the level of knowledge, it should be considered that factors other than the eight examined here also contribute to variation in the level of knowledge. For example, only 29.1 per cent of the variation in knowledge has been accounted for by the eight variables in Azamgarh. This means that there are other important sources through which members of a pre-literate, backward community, such as Azamgarh, assimilate knowledge. The important sources of communication in such societies are through traditional institutions and methods of communication, which primarily communicate traditional beliefs and values. Parents and kith and kin are also important sources through which ideas are assimilated. Such means of communication are outside the reach of modern science and knowledge, limiting the percolation of scientific knowledge and ideas in Azamgarh.

In Saharanpur, though modern institutions like mass media and education play a substantial role in increasing knowledge, 51.7 per cent of the source of variation in knowledge is unexplained. As in Azamgarh, this might have been the contribution of traditional sources and factors which were not examined. Similarly, in Trichur also, 58.5 per cent of the variation has not been explained by the eight variables examined here, indicating that other sources make important contributions to the variation in the level of knowledge. This may mean that knowledge is acquired through a variety of means. The finding that only a part of the total variance in knowledge has been explained by the independent variables may be an indication of the relative stability of empirical beliefs, constituting the outer layer of the cultural system.

Correlates of Variation in Components of Knowledge: Knowledge About Natural Phenomena

Regression analysis of the contribution of the independent variables to variation in each component of cognitive orientation was done. This has been done for all the respondents together, and separately for respondents from each of the blocks. In Table 6.2, the results of these analyses in respect to knowledge about natural phenomena are given. At the aggregate level (column 5), the R^2 value of 0.384 indicates that 38.4 per cent of the variance in this aspect of knowledge has been explained by the independent variables. The F value of 46.06 is highly significant at the 1 per cent level, indicating significant variations in the relative contribution of the independent variables. Among the eight variables, education of self, membership in associations, exposure to mass media, and value of inputs

Table 6.2

Results of Multiple Regression Analysis between Knowledge about Natural Phenomena and Socio-Economic Characteristics

Characteristics	Azamgarh (N = 200)	Saharanpur (N = 200)	Trichur (N = 200)	Aggregate (N = 600)
i	2	3	4	5
1. Father's education	0.501*	0.224	0.264	0.324
	(2.81)	(1.16)	(0.31)	(2.11)
2. Education of self	−0.104	0.516*	2.432†	0.775†
	(0.56)	(6.80)	(18.24)	(8.42)
3. Membership in associations	0.286*	−0.094	0.206	0.240*
	(3.33)	(0.61)	(0.70)	(2.18)
4. Exposure to mass media	0.012	0.345†	0.221*	0.341†
	(0.22)	(22.03)	(4.81)	(20.10)
5. Spatial mobility	0.048	0.057*	0.011	0.045*
	(2.33)	(3.83)	(0.26)	(1.87)
6. Types of tools used	−0.012	0.012	−0.059	−0.502†
	(0.11)	(0.03)	(0.06)	(1.06)
7. Value of inputs used	0.001†	0.000	0.002	0.001†
	(10.63)	(0.05)	(0.65)	(1.75)
8. Per capita monthly income	0.002	0.001	0.000	0.001*
	(1.37)	(1.83)	(0.02)	(0.84)
	$R^2 = 0.200$	$R^2 = 0.351$	$R^2 = 0.245$	$R^2 = 0.384$
	F = 5.97†	F = 12.92†	F = 7.75†	F = 46.06†

Note: Figures in brackets indicate percentage of variance explained by an independent variable.
† = $P < 0.01$; * = $P < 0.05$.

are significantly related to variation in knowledge at the 1 per cent level, while spatial mobility and per capita monthly income are related at the 5 per cent level of significance. Among these, the most important variable is exposure to mass media, which contributes 20.10 per cent to the total variation in knowledge. This is followed by education (8.42 per cent), membership in associations (2.18 per cent), spatial mobility (1.87 per cent), value of inputs (1.75 per cent), per capita monthly income (0.84 per cent) and father's education (2.11 per cent).

In the case of Azamgarh respondents, R^2 of 0.200 indicates that 20.0 per cent of the variation is explained. The F value is significant at the 1 per cent level, implying that variation in the relative contribution of the different independent variables is significant. The characteristics making significant contribution to the variation and their relative contribution are father's education (2.81 per cent), membership in associations (3.33 per cent) and value of inputs (10.63 per cent).

In the case of the Saharanpur respondents, the R^2 value of 0.351 indicates that 35.1 per cent of variation in knowledge about natural phenomena is explained. The F value of 12.92 is significant at the 1 per cent level, indicating a significant difference in the contribution of different independent variables. Characteristics which made a significant contribution to the variation are exposure to mass media (22.03 per cent), education (6.80 per cent) and spatial mobility (3.83 per cent).

In the case of Trichur respondents, the R^2 value is 0.245, indicating that 24.5 per cent of the variation in the knowledge about natural phenomena has been explained. The F value of 7.75 indicates a significant difference among the eight independent variables. Of these, education of the respondents is significantly related with variation in the level of knowledge, and it accounted for 18.24 per cent of the variation in knowledge about natural phenomena, followed by exposure to mass media accounting for 4.81 per cent of the variation. The contributions of all other independent variables to variation in knowledge about natural phenomena are less than 1 per cent.

The foregoing examination thus indicates that variation in exposure to mass media, education of self, father's education and spatial mobility are the main variables contributing to variation in knowledge about natural phenomena.

Knowledge about Soil and Plants

Another component of cognitive orientation examined is respondents' knowledge about plants and soil. In Table 6.3, the correlation coefficients of regression between the scores obtained by the respondents on knowledge about plants and soil and their socioeconomic characteristics, R^2 and F values are given. For the aggregate sample (column 5), R^2 is 0.316, indicating that 31.6 per cent of the total variance has been explained by the eight independent variables. The F ratio of 34.13 indicates significant variation in the

Table 6.3
Results of Multiple Regression Analysis between Knowledge about
Soil and Plants and Socio-Economic Characteristics

Characteristics 1	Azamgarh (N = 200) 2	Saharanpur (N = 200) 3	Trichur (N = 200) 4	Aggregate (N = 600) 5
1. Father's education	0.274	0.141	−0.176	0.146
	(1.77)	(0.99)	(0.12)	(1.74)
2. Education of self	−0.052	0.285	0.713†	0.337†
	(0.45)	(5.20)	(12.17)	(6.48)
3. Membership in				
associations	0.060	0.049	0.001	0.078
	(0.39)	(0.53)	(0.00)	(1.19)
4. Exposure to mass media	0.105†	0.120†	0.022	0.180†
	(5.74)	(18.46)	(0.73)	(20.05)
5. Spatial mobility	0.047*	0.009	−0.012	0.005
	(2.39)	(0.54)	(0.03)	(0.28)
6. Types of tools used	0.064	−0.257	0.356	−0.204*
	(0.57)	(0.22)	(2.78)	(0.84)
7. Value of inputs used	0.001	0.000	0.000	0.000
	(3.18)	(0.71)	(0.66)	(1.10)
8. Per capita monthly				
income	0.000	0.000	0.000	0.000
	(0.11)	(0.03)	(0.01)	(0.05)
	$R^2 = 0.137$	$R^2 = 0.267$	$R^2 = 0.165$	$R^2 = 0.316$
	F = 3.79†	F = 8.70†	F = 4.72†	F = 34.13†

Note: Figures in brackets indicate percentage of variance explained by an independent variable.
† = $P < 0.01$; * = $P < 0.05$.

relative contribution of the independent variables. Respondents' exposure to mass media and education are related to the variation in knowledge at the 1 per cent level of significance, accounting for 20.05 per cent and 6.48 per cent of the variation. The type of tools used is negatively related and contributed 0.84 per cent of the variation.

In the case of the Azamgarh respondents, the R^2 value of 0.137 indicates that only a relatively small proportion of 13.7 per cent of the total variance has been explained by the eight independent variables. However, the F value of 3.79, significant at the 1 per cent level, indicates that there is significant difference among the independent variables. Exposure to mass media and spatial mobility contributed 5.74 per cent and 2.39 per cent to the variation in knowledge. While father's education contributed 1.77 per cent to the variation, the value of inputs contributed 3.18 per cent to it.

In the case of the Saharanpur respondents, the R^2 of 0.267 indicates that 26.7 per cent of the variation has been explained. F value is significant at the 1 per cent level. Among the eight variables, only respondents' exposure to mass media is significantly related with the variation in knowledge, contributing 18.46 per cent to it. In the case of the Trichur respondents, R^2 of 0.165 indicates that 16.5 per cent of the variation has been explained. Among the eight variables, only respondents' education is significantly related with the variation in knowledge about soil and plants, contributing 12.17 per cent to the variation in it. Thus, it is respondents' exposure to mass media and education which significantly increases the level of their knowledge about soil and plants.

Agronomic Practices

In Table 6.4, the results of regression coefficients between the scores obtained by the respondents on the five items of knowledge about agronomic practices and their socio-economic characteristics, R^2 value and F value are given, jointly for all the respondents, and separately for respondents from each of the three areas. The R^2 value of 0.016 indicates that in the case of the aggregate sample, only 1.6 per cent of the variation has been explained. The F value of 1.20 is not significant, indicating that there is no significant variation in the contribution of the different independent variables to the variation of the dependent variable. The regression coefficients also indicate that none of the characteristics of the respondents is significantly related with variation in knowledge about agronomic practices.

In the case of the Azamgarh respondents, the R^2 value of 0.074 indicates that 7.4 per cent of the variation in the level of knowledge about agronomic practices has been contributed by the eight independent variables. The F value of 1.91 is not significant, indicating that the difference in the relative contribution of the independent variables to the variation in knowledge is not significant. The only characteristics significantly related with level of knowledge (at the 5 per cent level) are father's education (making

Table 6.4
Results of Multiple Regression Analysis between Knowledge about Agronomic Practices and Socio-Economic Characteristics

Characteristics	Azamgarh (N = 200)	Saharanpur (N = 200)	Trichur (N = 200)	Aggregate (N = 600)
1	2	3	4	5
1. Father's education	0.410* (1.94)	0.256 (1.87)	0.058 (0.48)	0.122 (0.43)
2. Education of self	--0.216* (1.93)	−0.039 (0.13)	0.058 (0.71)	−0.074 (0.12)
3. Membership in associations	0.008 (0.00)	−0.086 (0.45)	0.073* (1.39)	−0.051 (0.14)
4. Exposure to mass media	−0.040 (1.10)	0.084† (4.28)	0.052* (4.13)	0.007 (0.06)
5. Spatial mobility	−0.006 (0.20)	−0.014 (0.50)	0.005 (0.53)	−0.006 (0.09)
6. Types of tools used	0.150 (0.26)	0.012 (0.08)	−0.102 (0.54)	−0.041 (0.02)
7. Value of inputs used	0.000 (0.43)	0.000 (1.50)	0.003† (12.28)	0.000 (0.58)
8. Per capita monthly income	−0.002 (1.46)	0.001 (1.17)	0.000 (0.53)	0.000 (0.20)
	$R^2 = 0.074$ $F = 1.91$	$R^2 = 0.096$ $F = 2.54^*$	$R^2 = 0.195$ $F = 5.75†$	$R^2 = 0.016$ $F = 1.20$

Note: Figures in brackets indicate percentage of variance explained by an independent variable.
† = $P < 0.01$; * = $P < 0.05$.

a contribution of 1.94 per cent) and education of self (making a contribution of 1.93 per cent). Exposure to mass media accounted for 1.10 per cent of the variation. These results indicate that in Azamgarh, there is not much variation in the level of knowledge about agronomic practices of the respondents along with the variation in their characteristics.

In the case of the Saharanpur respondents, the R^2 value of 0.096 indicates that 9.6 per cent of the variation in the knowledge of respondents about agronomic practices has been explained by the eight independent variables. The F value of 5.75, significant at the 1 per cent level, indicates that the contribution of different independent variables to the variation in the level of knowledge varied significantly. Among the eight independent variables, the only variable significantly related with the variation in knowledge about agronomic practices is respondents' exposure to mass media, which contributed 4.28 per cent to the total explained variation. Minor contributions are made by father's education (1.87 per cent), value of inputs (1.50 per cent) and per capita monthly income (1.17 per cent).

In the case of the Trichur respondents, the R^2 value of 0.195 indicates that 19.5 per cent of the variation in the score on knowledge about agronomic practices has been explained. The F value of 5.75 is significant at the 1 per cent level, indicating significant variations in the contributions of different independent variables. Among the eight variables, the value of inputs used by the respondents and their exposure to mass media are significantly related with the variation in knowledge, and contributed 12.28 per cent and 4.13 per cent to the variation.

The foregoing examination of the knowledge about agronomic practices prevailing among the respondents from the three areas indicates that both at the aggregate level and at the local level, there is not much variation in the level of knowledge along with the variation in the socio-economic characteristics of the respondents. This may be due to the fact that farmers acquire knowledge in this sphere mainly through traditional channels not examined here.

Elementary Technical Knowledge and Skill

Elementary technical knowledge and skill is another component of cognitive orientation which was examined. In Table 6.5, the correlation coefficients between the scores obtained on the 15 items of technical knowledge and skill and the eight characteristics of the respondents are given. The R^2 and F values of the regression are also given in the table. At the aggregate level, the R^2 value of 0.426 indicates that 42.6 per cent of the variation in the level of technical knowledge and skill has been explained by the independent variables. The F value of 54.83 is significant at the 1 per cent level, implying that the relative contribution of the independent variables to the variation in the dependent variable differed at the 1 per cent level of significance. Among the eight variables, respondents' education and exposure to mass media are related to variation in technical knowledge and skill at the 1 per cent level of

Table 6.5
*Results of Multiple Regression Analysis between Knowledge about
Elementary Technics and Skills and Socio-Economic Characteristics*

Characteristics 1	Azamgarh (N = 200) 2	Saharanpur (N = 200) 3	Trichur (N = 200) 4	Aggregate (N = 600) 5
1. Father's education	0.403 (3.76)	0.414 (2.82)	0.077 (0.31)	0.327* (3.13)
2. Education of self	0.290* (4.32)	0.646† (10.37)	1.937† (24.76)	0.796† (13.10)
3. Membership in associations	0.338* (4.12)	−0.017 (0.15)	0.207 (1.39)	0.145 (1.80)
4. Exposure to mass media	0.203† (14.82)	0.246† (16.14)	0.249† (10.62)	0.258† (21.02)
5. Spatial mobility	0.026 (0.67)	0.039 (2.71)	0.018 (0.85)	0.030* (1.70)
6. Types of tools used	0.012 (0.10)	−0.050 (0.13)	−0.129 (0.17)	−0.147 (0.19)
7. Value of inputs used	0.001* (5.22)	0.000 (0.39)	0.001 (0.52)	0.000 (1.12)
8. Per capita monthly income	0.000 (0.03)	0.000 (0.35)	0.001 (0.73)	0.001 (0.50)
	$R^2 = 0.330$ F = 11.76†	$R^2 = 0.325$ F = 11.50†	$R^2 = 0.390$ F = 15.27†	$R^2 = 0.426$ F = 54.83†

Note: Figures in brackets indicate percentage of variance explained by an independent variable.
† = $P < 0.01$; * = $P < 0.05$.

significance, while their fathers' education and spatial mobility are related to it at the 5 per cent level of significance. Among the significantly related variables, the contribution of exposure to mass media is the highest, making a contribution of 21.02 per cent to the total variation, followed by education of self (13.10 per cent), fathers' education (3.13 per cent) and spatial mobility (1.70 per cent). These results emphasise the importance of education and mass media to the variation in the level of technical knowledge and skill of the respondents.

In the case of the Azamgarh respondents, the R^2 value of 0.330 indicates that 33.0 per cent of the variation in the dependent variable is explained. The F value of 11.76 per cent is significant at the 1 per cent level. Among the eight independent variables, the characteristics related with the variation in technical knowledge score and their relative contribution are respondents' exposure to mass media (14.82 per cent), education (4.32 per cent), membership in associations (4.12 per cent) and value of inputs (5.22 per cent). In the case of the Saharanpur respondents, the R^2 0.325 indicates that 32.5 per cent of the variation is jointly explained by the eight independent variables. The F value of 11.50 is significant at the 1 per cent level, indicating that the contribution of different independent variables to the variation of the dependent variable is significant at the 1 per cent level. Among the eight characteristics of the respondents, their exposure to mass media and education are related to variation in knowledge at the 1 per cent level, and contributed, respectively, 16.14 per cent and 10.37 per cent to the variation. Father's education made a contribution of 2.82 per cent to the variation. In the case of the Trichur respondents, the R^2 value of 0.390 indicates that 39.0 per cent of the variation in the technical knowledge is explained by the eight independent variables. The F value of 15.27, significant at the 1 per cent level, indicates significant variation in the relative contribution of the independent variables to variation in technical knowledge and skill. Among the eight variables, education of respondents and their exposure to mass media are related to variation in the level of knowledge at the 1 per cent level, contributing 24.76 per cent and 10.62 per cent, respectively, to the variation in knowledge and skill. Respondents' membership in associations contributed 1.39 per cent to the variation in knowledge. On the basis of these results, it can be concluded that the main factors responsible for the variation in the level of technical knowledge and skill of the respondents are their education and exposure to mass media.

Knowledge about Livestock Practices

In Table 6.6, the correlation coefficients of regression between the scores obtained by the respondents on the twelve items of knowledge about livestock practices (dependent variable) and the eight independent variables, the R^2 and F values of the regression are given. At the aggregate level, the R^2 value is 0.317, indicating that 31.7 per cent of the variation in the dependent variable (knowledge about livestock practices score) has been explained by the eight

Table 6.6

Results of Multiple Regression Analysis between Knowledge about
Livestock Practices and Socio-Economic Characteristics

Characteristics	Azamgarh (N = 200)	Saharanpur (N = 200)	Trichur (N = 200)	Aggregate (N = 600)
1	2	3	4	5
1. Father's education	−0.145	0.492*	0.033	0.267*
	(0.54)	(4.92)	(0.19)	(3.19)
2. Education of self	0.305	0.155	0.302*	0.243†
	(2.87)	(2.43)	(4.32)	(4.11)
3. Membership of associations	0.280	0.232*	0.074	0.208*
	(2.01)	(4.24)	(0.86)	(3.73)
4. Exposure to mass media	0.195†	0.178†	0.087†	0.188†
	(9.46)	(14.53)	(5.90)	(19.4)
5. Spatial mobility	0.100†	0.012	0.014	0.012
	(4.54)	(0.23)	(1.51)	(0.64)
6. Types of tools used	0.123	0.134	−0.113	−0.105
	(0.40)	(0.72)	(0.14)	(0.27)
7. Value of inputs used	0.000	0.000	0.000	0.000
	(0.27)	(0.61)	(1.85)	(0.35)
8. Per capita monthly income	−0.004*	−0.001	0.001	0.000
	(0.80)	(0.08)	(1.35)	(0.01)
	$R^2 = 0.193$	$R^2 = 0.26$	$R^2 = 0.158$	$R^2 = 0.317$
	F = 5.71†	F = 8.43†	F = 4.48†	F = 22.32†

Note: Figures in brackets indicate percentage of variance explained by an independent variable.
† = $P < 0.01$; * = $P < 0.05$.

independent variables. The F value of 22.32, significant at the 1 per cent level, indicates that there is significant variation in the relative contribution of the independent variables. The characteristics making significant contribution to variation in knowledge are respondents' exposure to mass media (19.4 per cent), education of self (4.11 per cent), membership in associations (3.73 per cent) and fathers' education (3.19 per cent). Thus, the most important cause of variation in the level of knowledge about livestock practices of the respondents is their exposure to mass media.

In the case of the Azamgarh respondents, the R^2 value of 0.193 indicates that 19.3 per cent of the variation in the score on knowledge about livestock practices is explained. The F value of 5.71 is significant at the 1 per cent level. Among the eight independent variables, exposure to mass media and spatial mobility are related with variation in the dependent variable at the₁1 per cent level, while per capita monthly income is related to it at the 5 per cent level. Their relative contributions to the variation of the dependent variable are 9.46 per cent, 4.54 per cent and 0.80 per cent. Among other characteristics, respondents' education makes a contribution of 2.87 per cent and membership in associations 2.01 per cent to the variation in the level of knowledge about livestock practices. In the case of the Saharanpur respondents, the regressions gave an R^2 of 0.26, indicating that 26 per cent of the variation in the dependent variable has been explained. The F value of 8.43 indicates that there is a significant difference in the relative contribution of the independent variables. Among these, exposure to mass media contributes 14.53 per cent to the variation in the level of knowledge, father's education 4.92 per cent, and membership in associations 4.24 per cent. In the case of the Trichur respondents, the R^2 value of 0.158 indicates that 15.8 per cent of the variation in the knowledge about livestock practices is explained. The F value of 4.48 indicates that the relative contribution of the independent variables differ significantly. Among these, respondents' exposure to mass media contributes 5.90 per cent to the total variation in knowledge, and education 4.32 per cent. These results indicate that exposure to mass media and education of the respondents are the main contributors to variation in knowledge about livestock practices.

Knowledge about Nutrition and Health

In Table 6.7, the coefficients of regression between the scores on the eight items of knowledge about nutrition and health (dependent variable) and the eight socio-economic characteristics (independent variables) of the respondents are given. The R^2 value of 0.232 obtained by the aggregate group of respondents (N = 600) indicates that the independent variables explained 23.2 per cent of the variation in the level of knowledge about nutrition and health. The F value of 22.32 is significant at the 1 per cent level, indicating that there is significant difference in the relative contribution of the independent variables. Among the eight independent variables,

Table 6.7
*Results of Multiple Regression Analysis between Knowledge about
Nutrition and Health and Socio-Economic Characteristics*

Characteristics	Azamgarh (N = 200)	Saharanpur (N = 200)	Trichur (N = 200)	Aggregate (N = 600)
1	2	3	4	5
1. Father's education	0.110	0.361*	0.151	0.249†
	(0.69)	(4,22)	(1.41)	(3.68)
2. Education of self	0.137	0.416†	0.660†	0.374†
	(1.69)	(9.87)	(12.57)	(8.51)
3. Membership in associations	0.142	−0.073	−0.066	−0.011
	(1.57)	(0.72)	(0.01)	(0.14)
4. Exposure to mass media	0.037	0.178†	0.072*	0.100†
	(1.34)	(18.89)	(3.85)	(10.84)
5. Spatial mobility	0.056†	−0.010	0.011	−0.001
	(4.69)	(0.40)	(0.17)	(0.03)
6. Types of tools used	−0.117	0.077	0.040	−0.049
	(0.12)	(0.27)	(0.11)	(0.15)
7. Value of inputs used	0.000	0.000	0.000	0.000
	(0.56)	(0.14)	(0.13)	(0.08)
8. Per capita monthly income	0.001	0.000	0.000	0.000
	(0.17)	(0.04)	(1.23)	(0.12)
	$R^2 = 0.103$	$R^2 = 0.32$	$R^2 = 0.189$	$R^2 = 0.232$
	$F = 2.74†$	$F = 11.24†$	$F = 5.57†$	$F = 22.32†$

Note: Figures in brackets indicate percentage of variance explained by an independent variable.
† = $P < 0.01$; * = $P < 0.05$.

fathers' education, education of self and exposure to mass media
are related to the variation in the knowledge score at the 1 per cent
level of significance. Among these, respondents' exposure to mass
media contributed 10.84 per cent to the variation in the level of
knowledge, education of self 8.51 per cent and father's education
3.68 per cent.

In the case of the Azamgarh respondents, the R^2 of 0.103
indicates that 10.3 per cent of the variation in the dependent
variable is explained. The F value of 2.74 is significant at the 1 per
cent level. Among the eight socio-economic characteristics, only
spatial mobility of the respondents is significantly related with

variation in knowledge about nutrition and health, making a contribution of 4.69 per cent to the variation. In the case of the Saharanpur respondents, the R^2 value of the regression is 0.32, indicating that 32.0 per cent of the variation in the level of knowledge about nutrition and health has been explained. The F value of 11.24 is significant at the 1 per cent level. Among the eight independent variables, respondents' education and exposure to mass media are related to the level of knowledge at the 1 per cent level, while fathers' education is related at the 5 per cent level, and their relative contribution to the variation in level of knowledge are 9.87 per cent, 18.89 per cent and 4.22 per cent. In the case of the Trichur respondents, the R^2 value of 0.189 indicates that 18.9 per cent of the variation in this aspect of knowledge has been explained. Respondents' education and exposure to mass media contribute 12.57 per cent and 3.85 per cent to the variation. Thus, it is exposure to mass media and education of the respondents which mainly contribute to the variation in knowledge about nutrition and health matters.

Causation of Diseases

In Table 6.8, the coefficient of regression between the scores obtained on the seventeen items enquiring about the level of knowledge of the respondents about the causation of diseases and their socio-economic characteristics are given. At the aggregate level, the R^2 of 0.344 indicates that 34.4 per cent of the variation in the level of knowledge of the respondents is explained by the eight independent variables. The F value of 38.74 is significant at the 1 per cent level, indicating that the relative contribution of the independent variables to the variation in socio-personal characteristics differs significantly. Among the eight characteristics of the respondents, the characteristics significantly related to variation in level of knowledge and their relative contributions are as follows: fathers' education (5.27 per cent), membership in associations (3.67 per cent), exposure to mass media (17.79 per cent), types of tools used (3.06 per cent) and the value of inputs used in agricultural production (1.87 per cent). Thus, as in other aspects of knowledge, the most important factor contributing to the level of knowledge of the respondents about the causation of diseases is their exposure to mass media.

Table 6.8

*Results of Multiple Regression Analysis between Knowledge about
the Cause of Diseases and Socio-Economic Characteristics*

Characteristics	Azamgarh (N = 200)	Saharanpur (N = 200)	Trichur (N = 200)	Aggregate (N = 600)
1	2	3	4	5
1. Father's education	−0.108	0.266	0.174	0.629†
	(0.05)	(2.20)	(0.61)	(5.27)
2. Education of self	0.033	−0.005	1.55†	0.268
	(0.11)	(0.06)	(13.54)	(2.68)
3. Membership in associations	0.242	−0.094	0.504†	0.337†
	(1.67)	(0.39)	(4.60)	(3.67)
4. Exposure to mass media	0.015	0.178†	0.164*	0.274†
	(0.12)	(16.64)	(4.77)	(17.79)
5. Spatial mobility	0.062*	0.007	0.018	0.004
	(2.81)·	(0.30)	(0.23)	(0.12)
6. Types of tools used	−0.038	−0.158	0.194	−0.714†
	(0.24)	(0.03)	(0.36)	(3.06)
7. Value of inputs used	0.001†	0.000	0.000	0.001†
	(7.14)	(1.59)	(0.28)	(1.87)
8. Per capita monthly income	0.002	0.000	0.000	0.000
	(0.78)	(0.08)	(0.01)	(0.03)
	R^2 = 0.123	R^2 = 0.201	R^2 = 0.239	R^2 = 0.344
	F = 3.35†	F = 6.61†	F = 7.50†	F = 38.74†

Note: Figures in brackets indicate percentage of variance explained by an independent variable.
† = $P < 0.01$; * = $P < 0.05$.

In the case of the Azamgarh respondents, the R^2 value of the
regression is 0.123, indicating that 12.3 per cent of the variation in
the level of knowledge about the causation of diseases has been
explained by the independent variables. Among these, spatial
mobility and the value of inputs are related to variation in the level
of knowledge, explaining 2.81 per cent and 7.14 per cent of the
variation. In the case of the Saharanpur respondents, the R^2 of
0.201 indicates that 20.1 per cent of the variation has been explained.
The F value of 6.61 is significant at the 1 per cent level. Among the
eight characteristics of the respondents, only their exposure to
mass media is significantly related with the level of knowledge,
making a contribution of 16.64 per cent to the total variation. In
the case of the Trichur respondents, the R^2 of 0.239 indicates that

23.9 per cent of the variation in the level of this aspect of know-ledge is explained. The F value of 7.50 is significant at the 1 per cent level. Among the eight characteristics, respondents' education and membership in associations are related with variation in knowledge at the 1 per cent level, and exposure to mass media at the 5 per cent level. Among these variables, education made the maximum contribution of 13.54 per cent, followed by membership in associations (4.60 per cent) and exposure to mass media (4.77 per cent). Thus, the main factors which contribute to variation in level of knowledge about the causation of diseases are exposure to mass media and education.

Knowledge about Human Fertility

In Table 6.9, the coefficients of regression between the scores obtained on the thirteen items examining the level of knowledge of respondents about fertility control practices and the eight independent variables are given. At the aggregate level, the R^2 value of 0.242 indicates that the eight independent variables jointly explained 24.2 per cent of the variation in the level of knowledge about fertility control. The F value of 23.59, significant at the 1 per cent level, indicates that the contribution of the independent variables to the variation of the dependent variable differed. Among the eight variables, respondents' education, membership in associations, exposure to mass media and fathers' education are significantly related to the variation in the level of knowledge, and contribute 4.37 per cent, 3.43 per cent, 11.41 per cent and 3.83 per cent to the variation.

In the case of the Azamgarh respondents, the R^2 of 0.135 indicates that 13.5 per cent of the variation in knowledge about fertility control practices has been explained. The F value of 3.73 is significant at the 1 per cent level. Among the eight characteristics, only exposure to mass media is significantly related to variation in knowledge, and contributes 5.11 per cent to the total variation.

In the case of the Saharanpur respondents, the R^2 of 0.185 indicates that 18.5 per cent of the variation in the level of knowledge about fertility control has been explained. The F value of 5.42 indicates that the relative contribution of the independent variables to the variation in knowledge differed at the 1 per cent level.

Table 6.9
*Results of Multiple Regression Analysis between Knowledge about
Human Fertility and Socio-Economic Characteristics*

Characteristics	Azamgarh (N = 200)	Saharanpur (N = 200)	Trichur (N = 200)	Aggregate (N = 600)
1	2	3	4	5
1. Father's education	0.633	0.216	−0.018	0.494†
	(3.26)	(0.77)	(0.06)	(3.83)
2. Education of self	0.339	0.494*	0.568*	0.409†
	(2.44)	(4.60)	(4.99)	(4.37)
3. Membership in associations	0.149	0.120	0.276*	0.306†
	(0.47)	(1.15)	(3.33)	(3.43)
4. Exposure to mass media	0.164†	0.059	0.264†	0.197†
	(5.11)	(1.39)	(14.74)	(11.41)
5. Spatial mobility	0.059	0.056*	−0.017	0.022
	(1.02)	(3.09)	(0.30)	(0.81)
6. Types of tools used	−0.161	0.999†	−0.440	−0.094
	(0.31)	(9.91)	(0.36)	(0.12)
7. Value of inputs used	−0.001	0.001	0.000	0.000
	(1.01)	(3.34)	(0.16)	(0.04)
8. Per capita monthly income	−0.001	0.001	0.000	0.000
	(0.07)	(0.90)	(0.31)	(0.18)
	$R^2 = 0.135$	$R^2 = 0.185$	$R^2 = 0.235$	$R^2 = 0.242$
	F = 3.73†	F = 5.42†	F = 7.34†	F = 23.59†

Note: Figures in brackets indicate percentage of variance explained by an independent variable.
† = $P < 0.01$; * = $P < 0.05$.

Among the eight characteristics of the respondents, their education, spatial mobility and types of tools used are significantly related with the variation in knowledge, contributing 4.60 per cent, 3.09 per cent and 9.91 per cent, respectively, to the variation in the level of knowledge.

In the case of the Trichur respondents, the R^2 value is 0.235, indicating that 23.5 per cent of the variation in the level of knowledge has been explained. The F value of 7.34 indicates that the relative contribution of the independent variables differed at the 1 per cent level. Among the eight variables, respondents' education, membership in associations and exposure to mass media are significantly related with the level of their knowledge about fertility control practices. Among these, exposure to mass media contributed 14.74 per cent to the variation in the level of knowledge, followed by education of respondents contributing 4.99 per cent, and membership in associations contributing 3.33 per cent. Thus, exposure to mass media and education are the most important variables which contribute to variations in the level of knowledge about birth control practices.

Concern with Philosophical and Moral Issues

Table 6.10 provides the regression results between the scores obtained on philosophical and moral issues and the socio-economic characteristics of the respondents. At the aggregate level, the R^2 value is 0.166, showing that 16.6 per cent of the variation in the dependent variable (concern with philosophical and moral issues) has been explained by the eight independent variables. The F value 14.71 is significant at the 1 per cent level. Among the independent variables, membership of associations and exposure to mass media are found to be significantly associated with the dependent variable at the 1 per cent level, contributing 3.23 per cent and 7.88 per cent to the total variation. Education of self showed a positive relation with philosophical and moral issues at the 5 per cent level, explaining 3.37 per cent of the total variation.

The total variance explained in the philosophical and moral issues of the Azamgarh respondents through their socio-economic characteristics amounted to 13.6 per cent. The F value of 3.76 is significant at the 1 per cent level. Among the socio-economic characteristics of the respondents, membership in associations and types of tools used for agricultural production showed positive associations with philosophical and moral issues at the 1 per cent level and 5 per cent level of significance, respectively. Membership of formal associations explained 4.79 per cent and types of tools used explained 3.61 per cent of the variations. The rest of the variables do not show any positively significant association with the dependent variable.

In the case of the Saharanpur respondents, the R^2 value of 0.297 accounted for 29.7 per cent of the variation in their philosophical and moral issues through the eight socio-economic characteristics.

Table 6.10

Results of Multiple Regression Analysis between Concern with
Philosophical and Moral Issues and Socio-Economic Characteristics

Characteristics 1	Azamgarh (N = 200) 2	Saharanpur (N = 200) 3	Trichur (N = 200) 4	Aggregate (N = 600) 5
1. Father's education	−0.150	0.175*	−0.046	0.077
	(0.73)	(3.71)	(0.09)	(1.17)
2. Education of self	0.151	0.084	0.275	0.139*
	(2.72)	(3.25)	(2.69)	(3.37)
3. Membership in associations	0.204†	0.138†	0.008	0.114†
	(4.79)	(7.27)	(0.04)	(3.23)
4. Exposure to mass media	0.048	0.043†	0.085*	0.060†
	(3.90)	(6.02)	(4.32)	(7.88)
5. Spatial mobility	−0.005	0.019†	−0.009	0.003
	(0.01)	(4.17)	(0.14)	(0.25)
6. Types of tools used	0.219*	0.197*	−0.246	−0.009
	(3.61)	(4.57)	(0.05)	(0.01)
7. Value of inputs used	0.000	−0.001*	0.000	0.000
	(0.76)	(2.79)	(1.99)	(0.61)
8. Per capita monthly income	0.000	0.001*	0.000	0.000
	(0.76)	(3.54)	(0.03)	(0.80)
	$R^2 = 0.136$	$R^2 = 0.297$	$R^2 = 0.089$	$R^2 = 0.166$
	$F = 3.76$†	$F = 10.09$†	$F = 2.33$*	$F = 14.71$†

Note: Figures in brackets indicate percentage of variance explained by an independent variable.
† = $P < 0.01$; * = $P < 0.05$.

The F ratio value of 10.09, significant at the 1 per cent level, shows
that the relative contribution of independent variables towards the
variation in the dependent variable differed significantly. Except
for education of self, all the independent variables showed significant associations with the dependent variable. Among the independent variables, membership in associations, exposure to mass
media and spatial mobility are significantly related with the
dependent variable at the 1 per cent level contributing 7.27 per
cent, 6.02 per cent and 4.17 per cent, respectively, to the total
variation. Among the other significant variables, types of tools,

education of father and per capita income showed a positive significant relation with the dependent variable at the 5 per cent level, while the value of inputs showed a negative association at the 5 per cent level with the dependent variable.

Among the Trichur respondents, the eight socio-economic characteristics could explain only 8.9 per cent of the variation in the dependent variable. Here, among the eight independent variables, only exposure to mass media showed a positive significant association with the dependent variables at the 5 per cent level.

The foregoing analysis indicates that the eight socio-economic characteristics of the respondents explained the very low percentage of variation in their philosophical and moral concerns. Among their socio-economic characteristics, exposure to mass media followed by membership in association are the important correlates of philosophical and moral concerns.

Summary

In this chapter, the relative contribution of the socio-economic characteristics of the respondents to the variation in the different dimensions of their cognitive orientation was examined through regression analysis. The eight socio-economic characteristics taken into consideration for this purpose were respondents' education, their fathers' education, membership in associations, exposure to mass media, spatial mobility, types of tools used, value of inputs used in agricultural production and per capita household income. The components of cognitive orientation, with reference to which this analysis was done, were knowledge about plants and soil; agronomic practices; technical knowledge and skill; livestock practices; nutrition and health; causation of diseases; fertility control; and concern with philosophical issues. The analyses were done at the aggregate level, for the whole (N = 600) sample, as also for a sample from each area. By and large, these analyses showed similar trends. Only a portion of the variation in the level of knowledge was explained by the eight independent variables, indicating that other variables not covered in the analyses also made substantial contribution to the variation in the level of knowledge. Among the eight characteristics of the respondents examined, exposure to mass media was found to be the most important factor contributing to variations in the level of knowledge. This was followed by education of the respondents, the education of their fathers, and their membership in associations. On the other hand, the contribution of types of tools used, value of inputs used in agricultural production and per capita household income to variation in the level of knowledge was random and weak, and sometimes the relations were negative.

7

Correlates of Values

In the previous chapter, the contribution of different socio-economic factors to the variations in the knowledge of the respondents was seen. In this chapter, the impact of socio-economic characteristics on variations in the value orientation of the respondents is examined.

The analyses to establish the relation between the pattern of value orientation and socio-economic characteristics have been done at different levels. First, the analysis has been done at the aggregate level, wherein the responses to the nine components of value orientation were jointly taken into consideration and treated as a dependent variable. These components are basic values; social values; values about human relations; values about agronomic practices; values about livestock farming; values about nutrition and health; values about fertility control; values about commercial activities; self-assessment; and aspiration for socio-economic advancement. The scores obtained by the respondents on the various items in the ten components were added to develop an index of aggregate value orientation. Further analyses were done at the level of each component of value orientation, treating the scores obtained by the respondents on each of the ten components as a dependent variable. Analyses were done, further, by aggregating the sample from the three areas into a single group (N = 600) and also separately for the sample of respondents from each area. As in the case of empirical knowledge, the analysis to examine the contribution of different variables to the variation in value orientation is done through multiple regression analyses. Through this analysis, it is estimated how much variation in the value orientation is explained by the independent variables, jointly and separately. For the purpose of interpreting the data, the value of multiple R (R^2), the relative contribution of independent variables, and the regression coefficients and F ratio are used. The R^2 gives the percentage of variance explained by the regression.

Correlates of Value Orientation

In Table 7.1, the results of regression between the aggregate value orientation score and the eight. independent variables (socio-economic characteristics) are given for the aggregate sample of 600 respondents, as also the sample from each area. In the case of the aggregate sample (column 5), the R^2 of 0.314 indicates that 31.4 per cent of the variation in value orientation has been explained by the eight characteristics. The F value of 33.82 indicates that the contribution of different factors to variation in value orientation differed at the 1 per cent level of significance.

Among the eight independent variables, father's education, education of self, membership in associations, and exposure to mass media are significantly related with the variation in value orientation. Among these, the most important variable is exposure to mass media, contributing 19.97 per cent to the total variation in value orientation, followed by education of self (4.49 per cent), fathers' education (3.17 per cent), and membership in associations (1.92 per cent). The total variance of value orientation explained by the eight variables (31.4 per cent) is considerably lower than the variance of 54.4 per cent of the cognitive orientation explained by the eight variables. The substantially larger variance of cognitive orientation explained indicates that the cognitive aspect of culture is prone to greater change, while value orientation is more stable.

In the case of the Azamgarh respondents, the R^2 of 0.203 indicates that 20.3 per cent of the variation in value orientation has been explained by the eight independent variables. The F value of 6.082, significant at the 1 per cent level, indicates significant variation in the contribution of independent variables. Among these, respondents' education, membership in assosications and exposure to mass media are significantly related to the variation in value orientation, contributing 6.38 per cent, 4.03 per cent and 4.83 per cent. Fathers' education contributes 2.79 per cent to the variation.

Table 7.1

Results of Multiple Regression Analysis between the Aggregate Index of Value Orientation Score and Socio-Economic Characteristics

Characteristics	Azamgarh (N = 200)	Saharanpur (N = 200)	Trichur (N = 200)	Aggregate (N = 600)
1	2	3	4	5
1. Father's education	1.885	3.410	0.720	2.176*
	(2.79)	(2.57)	(0.90)	(3.17)
2. Education of self	2.394*	0.296	3.815†	2.128†
	(6.38)	(0.35)	(10.22)	(4.49)
3. Membership in associations	1.935*	0.285	0.397	0.995*
	(4.03)	(0.27)	(0.62)	(1.92)
4. Exposure to mass media	0.558*	2.173†	0.815†	1.577†
	(4.83)	(16.77)	(9.12)	(19.97)
5. Spatial mobility	0.240	0.164	0.018	0.138
	(1.50)	(0.80)	(0.18)	(1.02)
6. Types of tools used	0.388	1.861	−1.012	−0.089
	(0.37)	(0.79)	(0.14)	(0.01)
7. Value of inputs used	0.001	−0.002	0.001	0.002
	(0.49)	(0.65)	(0.67)	(0.13)
8. Per capita monthly income	−0.005	0.004	0.001	0.004
	(0.13)	(0.44)	(0.35)	(0.66)
	$R^2 = 0.203$	$R^2 = 0.213$	$R^2 = 0.219$	$R^2 = 0.314$
	F = 6.082†	F = 6.46†	F = 6.7†	F = 33.82†

Note: Figures in brackets indicate percentage of variance explained by an independent variable.
† = $P < 0.01$; * = $P < 0.05$.

In the case of the Saharanpur respondents, the R^2 of 0.213 indicates that 21.3 per cent of the variation in value orientation is explained. The F value of 6.46 indicates a significant difference in the contributions of different independent variables. Among the eight characteristics of the respondents, only their exposure to mass media is significantly related with the variation, and it contributes 16.77 per cent to the variation in value orientation. Among the other variables, father's education contributes 2.57 per cent to the variation. In the case of the Trichur respondents, the R^2 of 0.219 indicates that 21.9 per cent of the variation in value orientation has been explained by the eight independent variables. The F value of 6.7 is significant at the 1 per cent level, indicating a significant difference in the relative contribution of different characteristics. Among the eight characteristics, respondents' education and exposure to mass media contribute 10.22 per cent and 9.12 per cent, respectively, to the total variation in value orientation. The analysis thus shows that both at the aggregate level and at regional level only a small portion of the variation in value orientation is explained by the independent variables. Compared to the extent of variation explained by the independent variables to change in knowledge, the extent of variation in value orientation explained by the variables is less, indicating the relative stability of the value orientation.

Basic Values

In Table 7.2, the correlation coefficients of regression between the scores obtained by the respondents on the eleven items pertaining to basic values and the eight socio-economic characteristics of the respondents are given. At the aggregate level (column 5), the R^2 value of 0.076 indicates that only 7.6 per cent of the variation in basic values is explained by the eight independent variables. The F value of 6.08 is significant at the 1 per cent level, indicating significant variation in the relative contribution of different characteristics. Among the eight variables, only exposure to mass media and education are related to the variation in value orientation, making contributions of 5.6 per cent and 1.98 per cent to the variation.

In the case of the Azamgarh respondents, the R^2 value of 0.131 indicates that 13.1 per cent of the variation in the basic value is explained. The F value of 3.60 is significant at the 1 per cent level, indicating a significant difference in the relative contributions of the independent variables. Among these, respondents' education and types of tools used are significantly related with the variation in value orientation, respectively contributing 6.18 per cent and 2.83 per cent to the variation. In the case of the Saharanpur respondents, the R^2 value of 0.160 indicates that 16.0 per cent of variation in value orientation is explained, and the F value of 4.55 indicates a significant difference in the contribution of the independent variables. Among these, only exposure to mass media is significantly related with variation in value orientation, accounting for 13.27 per cent of its variation. Father's education made a contribution of 2.44 per cent. In the case of the Trichur respondents,

Table 7.2
*Results of Multiple Regression Analysis between Basic Values
and Socio-Economic Characteristics*

Characteristics	Azamgarh (N = 200)	Saharanpur (N = 200)	Trichur (N = 200)	Aggregate (N = 600)
1	*2*	*3*	*4*	*5*
1. Father's education	0.145	0.504*	−0.388	0.057
	(0.43)	(2.44)	(1.23)	(0.23)
2. Education of self	0.824†	−0.247	0.398	0.280*
	(6.18)	(1.17)	(1.87)	(1.98)
3. Membership in associations	−0.118	0.126	−0.120	−0.006
	(0.19)	(0.89)	(0.12)	(0.03)
4. Exposure to mass media	−0.032	0.273†	0.112*	0.124†
	(0.13)	(13.27)	(2.54)	(5.06)
5. Spatial mobility	−0.070	0.005	−0.002	−0.016
	(1.89)	(0.08)	(0.02)	(0.09)
6. Types of tools used	−0.510*	0.098	−0.027	−0.123
	(2.83)	(0.32)	(0.03)	(0.18)
7. Value of inputs used	0.000	0.000	0.000	0.000
	(0.53)	(0.60)	(0.70)	(0.26)
8. Per capita monthly income	−0.003	0.000	−0.001	0.000
	(1.21)	(0.19)	(0.56)	(0.00)
	R^2 = 0.131	R^2 = 0.160	R^2 = 0.070	R^2 = 0.076
	F = 3.60†	F = 4.55†	F = 1.80	F = 6.08†

Note: Figures in brackets indicate percentage of variance explained by an independent variable.
† = $P < 0.01$; * = $P < 0.05$.

the R^2 of 0.070 indicates that 7.0 per cent of the variation in the basic values has been explained by the eight independent variables. The F value of 1.80 is not significant, indicating that there is no significant variation in the relative contribution of different independent variables to the variation in the basic value. These findings indicate that basic values remain stable, in spite of wide variations in the personal characteristics.

Social Values

In Table 7.3, the correlation coefficients of regression between the scores obtained on the twenty-two items about social values and

Table 7.3
*Results of Multiple Regression Analysis between Social Values
and Socio-Economic Characteristics*

Characteristics	Azamgarh (N = 200)	Saharanpur (N = 200)	Trichur (N = 200)	Aggregate (N = 600)
1	2	3	4	5
1. Father's education	−0.016	0.636	0.273	0.695†
	(0.02)	(1.17)	(1.06)	(3.59)
2. Education of self	0.504	−0.196	−0.168	0.033
	(1.94)	(0.36)	(0.12)	(0.19)
3. Membership in associations	0.520*	−0.475	−0.010	0.032
	(2.95)	(1.07)	(0.30)	(0.13)
4. Exposure to mass media	−0.064	0.446†	0.133*	0.327†
	(0.18)	(10.06)	(2.98)	(13.34)
5. Spatial mobility	−0.003	0.000	0.009	0.006
	(0.00)	(0.00)	(0.22)	(0.09)
6. Types of tools used	−0.037	0.165	−0.388	−0.724†
	(1.95)	(0.25)	(0.84)	(3.23)
7. Value of inputs used	−0.001	−0.001	0.000	0.000
	(1.39)	(0.47)	(0.01)	(0.02)
8. Per capita monthly income	−0.002	−0.002	0.000	−0.001
	(0.17)	(1.08)	(0.08)	(0.04)
	$R^2 = 0.067$	$R^2 = 0.132$	$R^2 = 0.050$	$R^2 = 0.206$
	$F = 1.71$	$F = 3.63†$	$F = 1.26$	$F = 19.17†$

Note: Figures in brackets indicate percentage of variance explained by an independent variable.
† = $P < 0.01$; * = $P < 0.05$.

the eight independent variables are given. At the aggregate level, the R^2 value of 0.206 indicates that 20.6 per cent of the variation in social values is explained by the eight independent variables. The F value of 19.17, significant at the 1 per cent level, indicates that the contribution of the independent variables to the variation of the dependent variable differed significantly. Among the eight variables, father's education, exposure to mass media and types of tools used are significantly related with variation in social values, contributing 3.59 per cent, 13.34 per cent and 3.23 per cent to it.

In the case of the Azamgarh respondents, the R^2 value is 0.067, indicating that only 6.7 per cent of the variation has been explained by the independent variables. The F value of 1.71 is not significant, indicating that the variation in the socio-economic characteristics of the respondents do not make a significant difference in the variation of their value orientation. Among the various characteristics of the respondents, only their membership in associations is significantly related with the variation in values, contributing 2.95 per cent to the variation in value orientation.

In the case of the Saharanpur respondents, R^2 of 0.132 indicates that 13.2 per cent of the variation in value orientation is explained. The F value of 3.63 is significant at the 1 per cent level, indicating a significant difference in the relative contribution of different independent variables. Among these, exposure to mass media makes a contribution of 10.06 per cent to the variation in values. Father's education contributed 1.17 per cent to the variation, while membership in associations made a contribution of 1.07. Thus, it is exposure to mass media which creates some change in the value orientation of the Saharanpur respondents.

In the case of the Trichur respondents, the R^2 value is 0.050, indicating that only 5.0 per cent of the variation in the value orientation of the respondents is explained by the independent variables. The F value of 1.26 is not significant, indicating no difference in the values along with the variation in socio-economic characteristics. Among the eight socio-economic characteristics, only exposure to mass media is significantly related to the variation in values, contributing 2.98 per cent to the variation in the values. These results indicate the relative stability of social values, despite variation in socio-economic characteristics. Both in Azamgarh, where the most conservative values prevail, and in Trichur, where value orientation is the most modern, variation in the socio-economic characteristics of respondents makes little difference to their value orientation. This means that values constitute a relatively stable aspect of the belief system, being little influenced by variations in socio-economic characteristics.

Values about Human Relations

In Table 7.4, the coefficients of regression between the scores of fifteen items enquiring about the values of the respondents regarding human relations and their eight socio-economic characteristics are given. At the aggregate level, the R^2 of 0.132 indicates that 13.2 per cent of the variation in values about human relations has

Table 7.4
Results of Multiple Regression Analysis between Values about
Human Relations and Socio-Economic Characteristics

Characteristics	Azamgarh (N = 200)	Saharanpur (N = 200)	Trichur (N = 200)	Aggregate (N = 600)
1	2	3	4	5
1. Father's education	0.320	0.122	−0.503†	−0.080
	(1.32)	(0.32)	(2.92)	(0.36)
2. Education of self	0.177	0.001	0.485*	0.249*
	(1.25)	(0.01)	(2.57)	(2.32)
3. Membership in associations	−0.136	−0.199	0.002	−0.032
	(0.01)	(0.08)	(0.00)	(0.16)
4. Exposure to mass media	0.081	0.190†	0.064	0.172†
	(2.22)	(7.08)	(1.14)	(9.92)
5. Spatial mobility	0.061	0.027	0.000	0.024
	(2.28)	(0.86)	(0.00)	(0.98)
6. Types of tools used	−0.123	0.217	−0.057	−0.137
	(0.08)	(0.40)	(0.01)	(0.48)
7. Value of inputs used	0.000	−0.001	0.000	0.000
	(0.00)	(1.15)	(0.02)	(0.02)
8. Per capita monthly income	0.002	0.000	0.000	0.000
	(0.73)	(0.02)	(0.52)	(0.03)
	$R^2 = 0.080$	$R^2 = 0.091$	$R^2 = 0.071$	$R^2 = 0.132$
	$F = 2.08*$	$F = 2.39*$	$F = 1.83$	$F = 11.24†$

Note: Figures in brackets indicate percentage of variance explained by an independent variable.
† = $P < 0.01$; * = $P < 0.05$.

been explained by the eight characteristics. The F value of 11.24 indicates that the relative contributions of different characteristics to the variation in value orientation differed. Among these, respondents' exposure to mass media and education are significantly related with the variation in value orientation, respectively contributing 9.92 per cent and 2.32 per cent to it.

In the case of the Azamgarh respondents, the R^2 of 0.080 indicates that only 8.0 per cent of the variation is explained. The F value of 2.08 is significant at the 5 per cent level. However, none of the eight characteristics is significantly related with the variation in values. In the case of the Saharanpur respondents, the R^2 value of 0.091 indicates that 9.1 per cent of the variation in values is explained. The F value of 2.39 is significant at the 5 per cent level. However, among the eight characteristics, only exposure to mass media is significantly related to variation in values, contributing 7.08 per cent to the variation. In the case of the Trichur respondents, the R^2 of 0.071 indicates that only 7.1 per cent of the variation in values about human relations is explained by the eight independent variables. The F value of 1.83 is not significant, indicating no significant variation in value orientation along with variations in socio-economic characteristics. Thus, as in the case of other aspects of value orientation, values about human relations are also not influenced much by variations in socio-economic characteristics, implying their relative stability.

Values about Agronomic Practices

In Table 7.5, the coefficients of regression between the scores on the four items enquiring about respondents' values about agronomic practices and their eight socio-economic characteristics are given. In the case of the aggregate sample, the R^2 of 0.123 indicates that 12.3 per cent of the variation in values about agronomic practices is explained by the independent variables. The F value of 10.36 indicates that the relative contribution of different independent variables differed significantly. Among the eight characteristics, only exposure to mass media is significantly related with variation in values, contributing 11.44 per cent to the variation in value orientation.

The regression results of the Azamgarh respondents give an R^2 value of 0.115, indicating that 11.5 per cent of the variation in values about agronomic practices is explained. The F value is significant at the 1 per cent level. Among the independent variables, exposure to mass media is significantly associated with the dependent variable, explaining 5.3 per cent of the variation. Four of the independent variables show a negative relation with the values regarding agronomic practices; of them, the value of inputs used for agriculture showed a significant negative association with the dependent variable at the 5 per cent level.

In the case of the Saharanpur respondents, the R^2 of 0.098 indicates that 9.8 per cent of the variation in values is explained by the eight independent variables. The F value of 2.59, significant at

Table 7.5

Results of Multiple Regression Analysis between Values about
Agronomic Practices and Socio-Economic Characteristics

Characteristics	Azamgarh (N = 200)	Saharanpur (N = 200)	Trichur (N = 200)	Aggregate (N = 600)
1	*2*	*3*	*4*	*5*
1. Father's education	−0.202	0.012	−0.005	−0.001
	(1.36)	(0.06)	(0.01)	(0.01)
2. Education of self	−0.151	0.010	0.098	0.030
	(1.86)	(0.12)	(1.40)	(0.43)
3. Membership in associations	0.036	0.013	0.029	0.026
	(0.01)	(0.01)	(0.21)	(0.41)
4. Exposure to mass media	0.076†	0.087†	0.010	0.080†
	(5.30)	(9.13)	(0.31)	(11.44)
5. Spatial mobility	0.006	0.001	−0.003	−0.001
	(0.09)	(0.02)	(0.00)	(0.03)
6. Types of tools used	0.118	−0.081	0.118	−0.082
	(0.06)	(0.47)	(0.80)	(0.81)
7. Value of inputs used	−0.001*	0.000	0.000	0.000
	(2.25)	(0.02)	(0.03)	(0.00)
8. Per capita monthly income	−0.001	0.000	0.001*	0.000
	(0.77)	(0.19)	(2.28)	(0.13)
	$R^2 = 0.115$	$R^2 = 0.098$	$R^2 = 0.046$	$R^2 = 0.123$
	$F = 3.10†$	$F = 2.59*$	$F = 1.15$	$F = 10.36†$

Note: Figures in brackets indicate percentage of variance explained by an independent variable.
† = $P < 0.01$; * = $P < 0.05$.

the 5 per cent level, indicates that the contribution of different
variables to the variation of the values differed significantly. However, among the eight characteristics of the respondents, only
exposure to mass media is significantly related with variation in
values, contributing 9.13 per cent to it. In the case of the Trichur
respondents, the R^2 value of 0.046 indicates that only 4.6 per cent
of the variation in values is explained. The F value of 1.15 indicates
that there is no significant difference in the relative contribution of
different variables to variation in values. The only characteristic
significantly related with the variation in values of the respondents
is per capita income, making a contribution of 2.28 per cent. These
results indicate that as in other aspects of value orientation, the

influence of socio-economic characteristics on variation in values about agronomic practices is nominal.

Values about Livestock Farming

In Table 7.6, the correlation coefficients of regression between the scores on the twelve items about respondents' values about livestock farming and their eight socio-economic characteristics are given. In the case of the aggregate sample, the R^2 of 0.236 indicates that 23.6 per cent of the variation in values about livestock farming is explained. Among these, respondents' exposure to mass media

Table 7.6
Results of Multiple Regression Analysis between Values about Livestock Farming and Socio-Economic Characteristics

Characteristics	Azamgarh (N = 200)	Saharanpur (N = 200)	Trichur (N = 200)	Aggregate (N = 600)
1	2	3	4	5
1. Father's education	−0.010	0.013	0.032	0.310*
	(0.01)	(0.03)	(0.07)	(2.68)
2. Education of self	−0.174	0.089	0.290	0.056
	(0.38)	(0.60)	(1.70)	(0.57)
3. Membership in associations	0.036	−0.189	−0.079	0.058
	(0.04)	(0.10)	(0.13)	(0.51)
4. Exposure to mass media	0.015	0.193†	0.059	0.224†
	(0.02)	(9.21)	(1.38)	(17.34)
5. Spatial mobility	0.046	0.019	0.000	0.019
	(1.76)	(0.65)	(0.00)	(0.77)
6. Types of tools used	0.152	0.277	0.082	−0.306
	(0.24)	(0.32)	(0.04)	(1.76)
7. Value of inputs used	0.000	0.000	0.000	0.000
	(0.05)	(0.03)	(0.56)	(0.00)
8. Per capita monthly income	0.002	0.001	−0.001	0.000
	(1.15)	(0.67)	(2.40)	(0.00)
	$R^2 = 0.037$	$R^2 = 0.115$	$R^2 = 0.063$	$R^2 = 0.236$
	$F = 0.92$	$F = 3.10†$	$F = 1.61$	$F = 22.82†$

Note: Figures in brackets indicate percentage of variance explained by an independent variable.
† = P < 0.01; * = P < 0.05.

is related to the variation in value orientation at the 1 per cent level of significance, while father's education is related to it at the 5 per cent level, and contributes 17.34 per cent and 2.68 per cent to the variation in value orientation.

In the case of the Azamgarh respondents, the R^2 of 0.037 indicates that only 3.7 per cent of the variation in this aspect of values is explained. The F value of 0.92 is not significant, indicating that respondents with different characteristics hold more or less similar values about livestock activities. In the case of the Saharanpur respondents, the R^2 value of 0.115 indicates that 11.5 per cent of the variation in values about livestock activities is explained by the independent variables. The F value of 3.10 is significant at the 1 per cent level. Among the eight variables, only exposure to mass media is significantly related to variation in values, contributing 9.21 per cent to the variation. In the case of the Trichur respondents, the R^2 of 0.063 indicates that 6.3 per cent of the variation in value orientation is explained by the eight independent variables. The F value of 1.61 is not significant, indicating that there is no significant variation in the value orientation along with the variation in characteristics. These results show that there is only a small amount of change in value orientation about livestock practices due to the change in respondents' socio-economic characteristics.

Values about Nutrition and Health

In Table 7.7, the coefficients of regression between the scores obtained on the nine items enquiring the values of the respondents about nutrition and health matters and their socio-economic characteristics are given. At the aggregate level, the R^2 value of 0.120 indicates that only 12.0 per cent of the variation is explained by the eight independent variables. The F value of 10.08 indicates that there is significant difference in the relative contribution of the independent variables. Among the eight characteristics of the respondents, their education and exposure to mass media are significantly related with the variation in this dimension of value orientation, and contribute 3.37 per cent and 7.49 per cent to the variation.

In the case of the Azamgarh respondents, the R^2 value of 0.037 indicates that only 3.7 per cent of the variation in values about

Table 7.7
Results of Multiple Regression Analysis between Values about Nutrition and Health and Socio-Economic Characteristics

Characteristics 1	Azamgarh (N = 200) 2	Saharanpur (N = 200) 3	Trichur (N = 200) 4	Aggregate (N = 600) 5
1. Father's education	−0.010	0.213	−0.218	0.099
	(0.01)	(0.95)	(0.37)	(0.66)
2. Education of self	−0.174	0.078	0.711†	0.296†
	(0.38)	(0.60)	(6.37)	(3.37)
3. Membership in associations	0.036	−0.006	−0.067	0.001
	(0.04)	(0.03)	(0.13)	(0.00)
4. Exposure to mass media	0.015	0.167†	0.011	0.122†
	(0.02)	(7.96)	(0.13)	(7.49)
5. Spatial mobility	0.046	0.010	0.006	0.004
	(1.76)	(0.28)	(0.16)	(0.13)
6. Types of tools used	0.152	0.190	0.126	−0.071
	(0.24)	(0.45)	(0.12)	(0.17)
7. Value of inputs used	0.000	0.000	0.000	0.000
	(0.05)	(0.34)	(0.39)	(0.02)
8. Per capita monthly income	0.002	0.001	0.000	0.000
	(1.15)	(0.48)	(0.06)	(0.17)
	$R^2 = 0.037$	$R^2 = 0.103$	$R^2 = 0.077$	$R^2 = 0.120$
	F = 0.92	F = 2.74†	F = 1.99*	F = 10.08†

Note: Figures in brackets indicate percentage of variance explained by an independent variable.
† = $P < 0.01$; * = $P < 0.05$.

dietary and health practices is explained by the eight independent variables. The F value of 0.92 is not significant, indicating no variation in this aspect of value orientation along with the variation in socio-economic characteristics. In the case of the Saharanpur respondents, the R^2 value of 0.103 indicates that 10.3 per cent of the variation in value orientation is explained. The F value of 2.74 is significant at the 1 per cent level. Among the eight characteristics of the respondents, only their exposure to mass media is significantly related with variation in values, contributing 7.96 per cent to it. In the case of the Trichur respondents, the R^2 of 0.077 indicates that 7.7 per cent of the variation in dietary and health values is explained. The F value of 1.99 is significant at the 5 per cent level. Among the eight characteristics, only education is significantly related with variation in values, contributing 6.37 per cent to the variation. These results show that as in other aspects of value orientation, values about dietary matters also do not vary with variation in the socio-personal characteristics, and that they are relatively stable.

Values about Fertility Control

In Table 7.8, the coefficients of regression analyses between the scores obtained on the thirteen items about fertility control practices and the eight independent variables are given. At the aggregate

Table 7.8
Results of Multiple Regression Analysis between Values about Control of Fertility and Socio-Economic Characteristics

Characteristics	Azamgarh (N = 200)	Saharanpur (N = 200)	Trichur (N = 200)	Aggregate (N = 600)
1	2	3	4	5
1. Father's education	0.436	−0.090	−0.082	0.099
	(0.69)	(0.17)	(0.03)	(0.51)
2. Education of self	−0.073	0.026	0.650†	0.214
	(0.07)	(0.14)	(4.45)	(1.69)
3. Membership in associations	−0.113	−0.107	0.007	0.033
	(0.02)	(0.20)	(0.01)	(0.20)
4. Exposure to mass media	0.017	0.327†	−0.016	0.206†
	(0.05)	(14.97)	(0.12)	(10.85)
5. Spatial mobility	0.073	0.023	−0.006	0.022
	(1.72)	(0.06)	(0.06)	(0.73)
6. Types of tools used	−0.865†	−0.274	−0.237	−0.546†
	(3.60)	(0.18)	(0.06)	(2.46)
7. Value of inputs used	0.001*	0.000	0.000	0.003*
	(0.57)	(0.38)	(0.39)	(0.65)
8. Per capita monthly income	0.001	0.000	0.000	0.000
	(0.19)	(0.02)	(0.03)	(0.21)
	$R^2 = 0.068$	$R^2 = 0.160$	$R^2 = 0.048$	$R^2 = 0.173$
	F = 1.74*	F = 4.55†	F = 1.20	F = 15.46†

Note: Figures in brackets indicate percentage of variance explained by an independent variable.
† = $P < 0.01$; * = $P < 0.05$.

level, the R^2 of 0.173 indicates that the eight independent variables together explained 17.3 per cent of the variation in respondents' values about fertility control measures. The F value of 15.46 is significant at the 1 per cent level, indicating a significant difference in the contribution of different independent variables. Among the eight characteristics of the respondents, their exposure to mass media is significantly related with the variation in values about fertility control, contributing 10.85 per cent to the variation. Among the other characteristics, education of respondents made a contribution of 1.69 per cent to the variation. The types of tools used is negatively related. The contribution of other characteristics to the variation in values is very negligible.

In Azamgarh, the R^2 value is 0.068, indicating that only 6.8 per cent of the variation is explained by the eight socio-economic characteristics. The F value of 1.74 is significant at the 5 per cent level. Among the eight characteristics, only the types of tools used is significantly related to variation in values, contributing 3.60 per cent to the variation. In the case of the Saharanpur respondents, R^2 is 0.160 indicating that 16.0 per cent of the variation is explained. Among the eight variables, only exposure to mass media makes a significant contribution of 14.97 per cent to the variation in value. In the case of the Trichur respondents, the R^2 of 0.048 indicates that only 4.8 per cent of the variation in values is explained. The F value of 1.20 is not significant, indicating that there is no significant variation in the relative contribution of different independent variables. Among the eight characteristics of the respondents, only their education is significantly related with variation in values about fertility control, making a contribution of 4.45 per cent to the total variation. Thus, the examination indicates that values about fertility control are not much influenced by variation in the socio-economic characteristics of the respondents. This is equally true of Azamgarh where respondents' values about fertility control are very conservative, and in Trichur where their values are very modern.

Values about Commercial Activities

In Table 7.9, the regression coefficients examining the relation between the scores obtained on the fourteen items examining

Table 7.9
Results of Multiple Regression Analysis between Values about
Commercial Activities and Socio-Economic Characteristics

Characteristics 1	Azamgarh (N = 200) 2	Saharanpur (N = 200) 3	Trichur (N = 200) 4	Aggregate (N = 600) 5
1. Father's education	−0.160 (0.22)	0.525 (1.67)	0.087 (0.44)	0.141 (0.48)
2. Education of self	0.041 (0.02)	−0.323 (0.55)	0.400† (4.36)	−0.018 (0.07)
3. Membership in associations	0.322* (2.92)	−0.080 (0.06)	−0.090 (0.44)	0.004 (0.01)
4. Exposure to mass media	−0.175 (1.3)	0.276† (9.11)	0.011 (0.19)	0.103† (3.22)
5. Spatial mobility	−0.010 (0.01)	−0.011 (0.01)	0.006 (0.13)	−0.001 (0.01)
6. Types of tools used	0.274 (2.39)	−0.282 (0.25)	0.344 (1.58)	0.146 (0.13)
7. Value of inputs used	0.000 (2.15)	0.000 (0.12)	0.000 (0.98)	0.000 (0.02)
8. Per capita monthly income	−0.001 (0.25)	0.001 (0.35)	0.001† (3.49)	0.000 (0.01)
	$R^2 = 0.095$ $F = 2.51*$	$R^2 = 0.109$ $F = 2.92†$	$R^2 = 0.116$ $F = 3.13†$	$R^2 = 0.037$ $F = 2.84†$

Note: Figures in brackets indicate percentage of variance explained by an independent variable.
† = $P < 0.01$; * = $P < 0.05$.

the values about commercial activities and the socio-economic characteristics of the respondents are given. At the aggregate level, the R^2 of 0.037 indicates that only 3.7 per cent of the variation in this aspect of values is influenced by variation in socio-economic characteristics. The F value of 2.84 is significant at the 1 per cent level. However, among the eight characteristics of the respondents, only their exposure to mass media is significantly related with the variation in value orientation, making a contribution of 3.22 per cent to the variation.

In the case of the Azamgarh respondents, the R^2 value of 0.095 indicates that 9.5 per cent of the variation in commercial values is explained by the independent variables. The F value is significant at the 5 per cent level, indicating significant variation in the contribution of the independent variables. Among the eight variables, only respondents' membership in associations is significantly related with the variation in value orientation, contributing 2.92 per cent to the variation. This was followed by types of tools used, making a contribution of 2.39 per cent, and exposure to mass media making a contribution of 1.53 per cent. In the case of the Saharanpur respondents, the R^2 value of 0.109 indicates that 10.9 per cent of the variation in the value orientation is explained by the independent variables. The F value of 2.92 is significant at the 1 per cent level. Among the eight variables, only exposure to mass media is significantly related with value orientation, contributing 9.11 per cent to its variation. In the case of the Trichur respondents, the R^2 of 0.116 indicates that 11.6 per cent of the variation in the values about commercial activities is explained by the independent variables. The F value of 3.13 is significant at the 1 per cent level. Among the eight variables, respondents' education and per capita monthly income showed a positive association while value of inputs was negatively related with the variation in value orientation. Among these, education contributed 4.36 per cent to variation in the commercial values, followed by per capita monthly income making a contribution of 3.49 per cent, and value of inputs making a contribution of 0.98 per cent. Thus, as in the case of other aspects of value orientation, the values about commercial activities also show great stability, and are not much influenced by the variation in socio-economic characteristics.

Self-Assessment

In Table 7.10, the correlation coefficients of regression between the self-assessment scores of the respondents and their socio-economic characteristics are given. The R^2 in the case of the aggregate sample is 0.206, indicating that 20.6 per cent of the variance in self-assessment is explained by the independent variables. The F value of 19.17 indicates that the contributions of different independent variables in this respect differed significantly. Among the eight independent variables, respondents' fathers' education, exposure to mass media and types of tools used (negatively) are significantly related with the variation in self-assessment,

Table 7.10
*Results of Multiple Regression Analysis between Self-Assessment
and Socio-Economic Characteristics*

Characteristics	Azamgarh (N = 200)	Saharanpur (N = 200)	Trichur (N = 200)	Aggregate (N = 600)
1	2	3	4	5
1. Father's education	0.310	−0.097	1.098†	0.695†
	(0.56)	(0.17)	(4.91)	(3.59)
2. Education of self	0.354	0.471	0.682	0.033
	(1.05)	(2.82)	(2.50)	(0.19)
3. Membership in associations	0.364	0.754†	0.262	0.032
	(0.74)	(8.03)	(0.88)	(0.13)
4. Exposure to mass media	0.212*	0.190*	0.266*	0.327†
	(3.22)	(4.23)	(4.91)	(13.34)
5. Spatial mobility	0.023	0.041	−0.010	0.006
	(0.30)	(1.05)	(0.12)	(0.09)
6. Types of tools used	1.377†	0.713	−0.586	−0.724†
	(4.39)	(4.57)	(0.04)	(3.23)
7. Value of inputs used	−0.002*	0.000	0.000	0.000
	(0.09)	(0.53)	(1.21)	(0.02)
8. Per capita monthly income	−0.004	0.001	0.002†	−0.001
	(0.42)	(0.51)	(4.00)	(0.04)
	$R^2 = 0.103$	$R^2 = 0.205$	$R^2 = 0.183$	$R^2 = 0.206$
	$F = 2.74†$	$F = 6.16†$	$F = 5.35†$	$F = 19.17†$

Note: Figures in brackets indicate percentage of variance explained by an independent variable.
† = $P < 0.01$; * = $P < 0.05$.

and contribute 3.59 per cent, 13.34 per cent and 3.23 per cent to the variation.

In the case of the Azamgarh respondents, the R^2 value of 0.103 indicates that 10.3 per cent of the variation in self-assessment is explained by the independent variables. The F value of 2.74 is significant at the 1 per cent level. Among the eight variables, the types of tools used is related with the self-assessment score at the 1 per cent level, while exposure to mass media is related to it at the 5 per cent level, and contributed 4.39 per cent and 3.22 per cent to the variation. Value of inputs is negatively related and contributed 0.09 per cent to the variation. In the case of the Saharanpur respondents, the R^2 value of 0.205 indicates that 20.5 per cent of the variation in self-assessment is due to variation in the eight independent variables. The F value of 6.16 indicates that the contribution of different variables to variation in self-assessment differed significantly. Among the eight variables, membership in associations, types of tools used and exposure to mass media are significantly related to the self-assessment score, and contribute 8.03 per cent, 4.57 per cent and 4.23 per cent, respectively, to the variation. In the case of the Trichur respondents, the R^2 of 0.183 indicates that 18.3 per cent of the variation in self-assessment is explained. The F value of 5.35 indicates that the contribution of the independent variables differed significantly. Among the eight variables, respondents' fathers' education, exposure to mass media and per capita monthly income are significantly related with the variation in their self-assessment, making contributions of 4.91 per cent and 4.00 per cent to the variation in self-assessment. These examinations indicate that variation in the socio-economic characteristics of the respondents make only a small variation in their self-assessment, and it is caused mainly by the variation in their exposure to mass media.

Aspiration for Economic Advancement

In Table 7.11, the correlation coefficients of regression analyses between the scores obtained on the five items of aspiration towards economic advancement and the eight socio-economic characteristics are given. In the case of the aggregate sample, the R^2 of 0.170 indicates that 17.0 per cent of the variation in the aspiration for economic advancement is explained. The F value of 15.4, significant at the 1 per cent level, indicates that the variation in the relative contribution of different variables to the variation of aspiration differed. The variables significantly related with the variation in aspiration and their relative contribution to it are as follows: fathers' education (2.25 per cent), education of self (3.10 per cent), membership in associations (3.42 per cent), exposure to mass media (2.35 per cent), spatial mobility (1.46 per cent), types of tools used (2.44 per cent) and per capita monthly income (2.00 per cent).

In the case of the Azamgarh respondents, the R^2 of 0.312 indicates that 31.2 per cent of the variation in the level of aspiration of the respondents is explained by the eight characteristics. The F

Table 7.11
Results of Multiple Regression Analysis between Aspiration
for Economic Advancement and Socio-Economic Characteristics

Characteristics	Azamgarh (N = 200)	Saharanpur (N = 200)	Trichur (N = 200)	Aggregate (N = 600)
1	2	3	4	5
1. Father's education	0.809	1.597†	0.426	0.648*
	(2.55)	(5.87)	(2.22)	(2.25)
2. Education of self	0.741	0.406	0.269	0.582*
	(4.11)	(1.71)	(1.37)	(3.10)
3. Membership in associations	1.195†	0.369	0.472†	0.513†
	(7.15)	(1.94)	(5.32)	(3.42)
4. Exposure to mass media	0.329†	0.025	0.165*	0.109*
	(7.13)	(0.27)	(5.28)	(2.35)
5. Spatial mobility	0.135*	0.051	0.014	0.059*
	(2.53)	(0.98)	(0.55)	(1.46)
6. Types of tools used	0.299	0.838	−0.389	0.790†
	(1.20)	(2.68)	(0.01)	(2.44)
7. Value of inputs used	0.002*	−0.001	0.001*	0.000
	(6.10)	(1.31)	(2.82)	(0.03)
8. Per capita monthly income	0.002	0.003*	0.009	0.002†
	(0.41)	(2.89)	(1.59)	(2.00)
	$R^2 = 0.312$	$R^2 = 0.150$	$R^2 = 0.190$	$R^2 = 0.170$
	$F = 10.83$†	$F = 4.21$†	$F = 5.60$†	$F = 15.4$†

Note: Figures in brackets indicate percentage of variance explained by an independent variable.
† = $P < 0.01$; * = $P < 0.05$.

value of 10.83 is significant at the 1 per cent level. The characteristics significantly related with the variation in aspiration and their contribution to it are as follows: exposure to mass media (7.13 per cent), membership in associations (7.15 per cent), spatial mobility (2.53 per cent) and value of inputs (6.10 per cent). In the case of the Saharanpur respondents, the R^2 of 0.150 indicates that 15.0 per cent of the variation in aspiration is explained by the independent variables. The F value of 4.21 is significant at the 1 per cent level. Among the eight characteristics of the respondents, only their fathers' education and per capita monthly income are significantly related with the variation of aspiration, and contributed, respectively, 5.87 per cent and 2.89 per cent to it. In the case of the Trichur respondents, the R^2 value of 0.190 indicates that 19.0 per cent of the variation in level of aspiration is explained by the eight independent variables. The F value of 5.60 indicates that the contribution of different variables differed at the 1 per cent level of significance. Among the eight characteristics of the respondents, their membership in associations, exposure to mass media and value of inputs are significantly related with the variation in the level of aspiration, and contributed 5.32 per cent, 5.28 per cent and 2.82 per cent to the variation.

Summary

In this chapter, the results of regression analyses done to estimate the relative contribution of different socio-economic characteristics to the variation in the value orientation of the respondents were discussed. These analyses were done jointly for the aggregate sample of respondents, and separately for the respondents from each area. The analyses were also done jointly for the aggregate value orientation, combining the ten dimensions of value orientation, and separately for each of these dimensions. These analyses revealed considerable similarity in the variation of value orientation in different areas, and in different dimensions of value orientation. The analyses done for the aggregate value orientation indicated that only a small portion of the variation in value orientation was due to variation in the socio-economic characteristics of the respondents. Compared to the extent of variation in knowledge explained by the socio-economic characteristics, the variation in value orientation explained by these characteristics was small. The small variation explained by the socio-economic characteristics meant the relative stability of value orientation. More or less similar was the pattern of relation seen between each dimension of value orientation and the different socio-economic characteristics. The basic values of the respondents showed only a small degree of variation due to variations in socio-economic characteristics, indicating its relative stability. A similar stability was noticed in the case of social values, values about human relations, agronomic practices, livestock farming, nutrition and health, fertility control, commercial activities, self-assessment and aspiration for socio-economic advancement. The small amount of change in the value orientation of the respondents was mostly contributed by their exposure to mass media, and their and their fathers' education.

8

Inter-Relation between Cognitive and Evaluative Dimensions

In the two earlier chapters, the factors contributing to variations in cognitive and value orientations were examined. It was seen that along with changes in socio-personal characteristics, cognitive orientation changed more than value orientation. In this chapter, the influence of knowledge, or the cognitive orientation of the respondents, on their value orientation is examined.

Correlates of Value Orientation

Value orientation and cognitive orientation are two important dimensions of any belief system. Social values have an empirical basis, necessitating changes in it along with changes in knowledge. The principle of pattern consistency also necessitates transformation in values, along with change in knowledge, as certain values become inconsistent with advances in knowledge. Therefore, the relation between cognitive orientation and value orientation warrants further analysis.

For understanding the relation between cognitive and value orientations, the correlations between the overall index of value orientation and the scores on different components of cognitive orientation were obtained. In Table 8.1, the coefficients of the correlations are given area-wise and at the aggregate level. It is seen that various components of cognitive orientation are highly

Table 8.1

*Coefficients of Correlation between Scores on Overall Index
of Value Orientation and Components of Cognitive Orientation*

Cognitive Orientation	Azamgarh (N = 200)	Saharanpur (N = 200)	Trichur (N = 200)	Aggregate (N = 600)
1. Knowledge about soil and plants	0.180	0.284†	0.257†	0.394†
2. Knowledge about natural phenomena	0.284†	0.246*	0.320†	0.419†
3. Elementary technical knowledge and skills	0.346†	0.473†	0.462†	0.516†
4. Knowledge about agronomic practices	−0.060	0.495†	0.082	0.234*
5. Knowledge related to livestock practices	0.384†	0.418†	0.130	0.485†
6. Knowledge about nutrition and health	0.331†	0.571†	0.130	0.490†
7. Knowledge about causation of diseases	0.263†	0.285†	0.016	0.406†
8. Knowledge about human fertility	0.290†	0.334†	0.061	0.394†
9. Concern with philosophical and moral issues	0.282	0.411†	−0.010	0.313
10. Aggregare index of cognitive orientation	0.479†	0.578†	0.469†	0.589†

Note: † = P < 0.01; * = P < 0.05.

related with value orientation in all the three areas, and at the aggregate level. Knowledge about soil and plants is highly correlated with the value orientation in Saharanpur, Trichur and for the aggregate sample. The scores on knowledge about natural phenomena and knowledge about elementary technical knowledge and skill are related with value orientation in all the areas. The value orientation scores are significantly related with the level of knowledge about agronomic practices, knowledge about livestock practices, knowledge about nutrition and health, knowledge about the causation of diseases, knowledge about fertility and fertility control measures, and concern with philosophical and moral issues in Azamgarh, Saharanpur, and at the aggregate level. The aggregate index of cognitive orientation also is highly related with the overall value orientation score in all the three areas, and at the aggregate level. These relations indicate that though the pattern of value orientation in each area has considerable autonomy and stability, it is strongly influenced by the variation in the level of knowledge about various activities prevailing in the three areas.

The correlation coefficients may be used as indices to estimate the relative influence of different components of cognitive orientation on value orientation. In the case of the Azamgarh respondents, the aggregate cognitive orientation score has the highest coefficient, indicating that variation in the level of knowledge directly contributes to change in value orientation. Among the various individual components of cognitive orientation, the highest coefficient is in the case of 'knowledge about livestock practices,' and 'elementary technical knowledge and skills'. Knowledge about 'nutrition and health matters' is the third important component highly correlated with variation in value orientation. The trend is similar in the case of the Saharanpur respondents also. In this case, the value of the correlation coefficient is the highest in the case of 'knowledge about nutrition and health' followed by 'knowledge about agronomic practices', 'elementary technical knowledge and skill,' and 'knowledge related to livestock practices'. In the case of the Trichur respondents, 'elementary technical knowledge and skill' shows the highest coefficient with the value orientation score. At the level of the aggregate sample also, 'elementary technical knowledge and skill' shows the highest degree of correlation with value orientation.

The high level of correlation observed between knowledge and value orientation indicates that expansion in knowledge is an important cause for change in values and individuals becoming modern and rational in their outlook. Earlier, it was seen that the main factors associated with change in cognitive orientation and value orientation were education and exposure to mass media. These factors not only change cognitive orientation, but the change in cognitive orientation makes further changes in value orientation. This means that though there is relative stability in value orientation, factors associated with socio-economic development (like exposure to mass media and expansion in knowledge) lead to rationalisation of values.

Having found that the pattern of value orientations of the respondents in each of the three areas, and at the aggregate level, are strongly correlated with the level of their knowledge, further analysis was done to estimate the contribution of different components of knowledge to change in values. For this purpose, a linear multiple regression was run, which indicated the degree of variance explained by each component of cognitive orientation to the variation in value. The score obtained on the overall index óf value orientation is the dependent variable, and the scores obtained on the various components of cognitive orientation are the independent variables. In Table 8.2 the results of this regression analysis are given.

In Column 5 of Table 8.2, the results of the regression for the aggregate sample are given. The R^2 value of 0.420 indicates that at the aggregate level, 42.0 per cent of the variance has been explained by the nine components of cognitive orientation (independent variables). The F value of 47.56, significant at the 1 per cent level, indicates that the relative contribution of different components of knowledge to variation in values differed significantly. Among the nine components of çognitive orientation, elementary technical knowledge and skill, knowledge related to livestock practices and awareness about nutrition and health are significantly related with variation in values. Among these, elementary technical knowledge and skill contributes 12.64 per cent to the variation in value orientation, followed by knowledge about livestock practices (10.19 per cent), knowledge about nutrition and health matters (9.29 per cent), and knowledge about agronomic practices (4.36 per cent). The contribution of other dimensions of knowledge to variation in value orientation is negligible.

In the case of the Azamgarh respondents, the R^2 of 0.293 indicates that 29.3 per cent of the variation in value orientation is explained by the nine components of cognitive orientation. The F value of 8.74 is significant at the 1 per cent level, indicating significant variation in the relative contribution of different components of cognitive orientation to variation in value orientation. Among the nine dimensions of knowledge, those significantly related with variation in value orientation and their relative contribution are as follows: respondents' technical knowledge and skill (7.00 per cent), knowledge about livestock practices (7.48 per cent), knowledge about nutrition and health (5.33 per cent), and concern with philosophical and moral issues (4.65 per cent). In the case of the Saharanpur respondents, the R^2 of 0.526 indicates that 52.6 per cent of the variation in value orientation is explained. The F value of 23.40 is significant at the 1 per cent level, indicating that the relative contribution of different components of cognitive

Table 8.2
Results of Multiple Regression Analysis between Overall Value
Orientation Scores and Components of Cognitive Orientation

Cognitive Orientation	Azamgarh (N = 200)	Saharanpur (N = 200)	Trichur (N = 200)	Aggregate (N = 600)
1	2	3	4	5
1. Knowledge about soil and plants	−0.780 (2.03)	−0.137 (0.36)	0.316 (1.19)	0.072 (0.36)
2. Knowledge about natural phenomena	0.586 (2.85)	−1.248* (4.51)	−0.070 (0.97)	−0.033 (0.31)
3. Elementary technical knowledge and skills	1.092† (7.00)	1.045 (6.51)	1.029† (14.63)	1.427† (12.64)
4. Knowledge about agronomic practices	0.173 (0.11)	5.010† (17.09)	1.064 (2.69)	2.581† (4.36)
5. Knowledge about livestock practices	0.976* (7.48)	1.744† (6.90)	0.786 (3.15)	1.710† (10.19)
6. Knowledge about nutrition and health	1.356* (5.33)	3.272† (15.67)	1.029* (5.03)	2.019† (9.29)
7. Knowledge about causation of diseases	0.290 (1.49)	0.731 (1.68)	0.113 (1.32)	0.125 (0.99)
8. Knowledge about human fertility	0.353 (2.59)	0.891* (4.30)	0.266 (1.89)	0.363 (2.58)
9. Concern with philosophical and moral issues	1.995* (4.65)	3.078* (5.30)	−0.379 (0.49)	0.956 (1.98)
	$R^2 = 0.293$ $F = 8.74†$	$R^2 = 0.526$ $F = 23.40†$	$R^2 = 0.284$ $F = 8.39†$	$R^2 = 0.420$ $F = 47.56†$

Note: Figures in brackets indicate percentage of variation explained by an independent variable.
† = $P < 0.01$; * = $P < 0.05$.

orientation differed significantly. Among the nine components of cognitive orientation, those which make significant contribution to change in value orientation are as follows: knowledge about agronomic practices (17.09 per cent), livestock practices (6.90 per cent), nutrition and health (15.67 per cent), human fertility (4.30 per cent), and concern with philosophical and moral issues (5.30 per cent). Knowledge about natural phenomena is negatively related with variation in value orientation and contributes 4.51 per cent to it. In the case of the Trichur respondents, the R^2 of 0.284 indicates that 28.4 per cent of the variation in value orientation is explained by the nine components of cognitive orientation. The F value of 8.39 is significant at the 1 per cent level. Among the nine components, elementary technical knowledge and skill and knowledge about nutrition and health are significantly related with variation in values, contributing 14.63 per cent and 5.03 per cent to the total variation in values. While knowledge about livestock practices makes a contribution of 3.15 per cent, knowledge about agronomic practices makes a contribution of 2.69 per cent. The foregoing examination indicates that four components of knowledge significantly contribute to variation in value orientation, namely, respondents' elementary technical knowledge and skill, knowledge about agronomic practices, knowledge about livestock practices, and knowledge about nutrition and health. These components of knowledge deal with immediate and day-to-day problems of the respondents, and it is variations in knowledge about them which greatly contribute to variation in their value orientation.

Basic Values

In Table 8.3, the coefficients of regression between the scores obtained on the nine components of cognitive orientation and the scores obtained on the eleven items of basic values, the relative contribution of independent variables, the R^2 and F values are given jointly for the whole sample, and separately for the sample from each area. At the aggregate level, the R^2 of 0.172 indicates that 17.2 per cent of the variation in basic values is explained by the nine components. The F value of 13.58 indicates that the relative contributions of different components of cognitive orientation to variation in basic values differed significantly. Among the nine components, elementary technical knowledge, knowledge about agronomic practices, livestock practices, nutrition and health, and concern with philosophical and moral issues are significantly related with variation in basic values, contributing 2.63 per cent,

Table 8.3
Results of Multiple Regression Analysis between Basic Value
and Components of Cognitive Orientation

Cognitive Orientation	Azamgarh (N = 200)	Saharanpur (N = 200)	Trichur (N = 200)	Aggregate (N = 600)
1	*2*	*3*	*4*	*5*
1. Knowledge about soil and plants	−0.484†	−0.197	0.041	−0.176*
	(4.79)	(1.91)	(0.30)	(1.48)
2. Knowledge about natural phenomena	−0.004	−0.155	0.032	−0.014
	(0.01)	(2.52)	(0.89)	(0.35)
3. Elementary technical knowledge and skills	−0.013	0.168*	0.072	0.095*
	(0.01)	(6.32)	(1.25)	(2.63)
4. Knowledge about agronomic practices	0.264	0.565†	−0.109	0.368†
	(1.22)	(11.17)	(0.06)	(3.45)
5. Knowledge about livestock practices	0.023	0.242*	0.167	0.163†
	(0.17)	(5.96)	(1.22)	(3.26)
6. Knowledge about nutrition and health	0.026	0.379†	0.058	0.268†
	(1.49)	(10.70)	(0.18)	(4.80)
7. Knowledge about causation of diseases	0.010	0.073	−0.077	−0.039
	(0.03)	(0.86)	(0.47)	(0.79)
8. Knowledge about human fertility	0.251†	0.058	−0.090	0.063
	(6.43)	(1.67)	(0.12)	(1.77)
9. Concern with philosophical and moral issues	0.321	0.440*	0.246	0.364†
	(1.56)	(4.80)	(2.59)	(3.88)
	$R^2 = 0.157$	$R^2 = 0.370$	$R^2 = 0.061$	$R^2 = 0.172$
	$F = 3.97$†	$F = 12.42$†	$F = 1.38$	$F = 13.58$†

Note: Figures in brackets indicate percentage of variation explained by an independent variable.
† = $P < 0.01$; * = $P < 0.05$.

3.45 per cent, 3.26 per cent, 4.80 per cent and 3.88 per cent, respectively, to the variation in values.

In the case of respondents from Azamgarh, the R^2 of 0.157 indicates that 15.7 per cent of the variation in the basic values is explained. The F value of 3.97 is significant at the 1 per cent level. Among the nine components of knowledge, those related to variation in value orientation and their relative contribution are as follows: knowledge about soil and plants is negatively related with variation in basic values, and contributes 4.79 per cent to the variation. Variation in knowledge about fertility control practices is positively related, and contributes 6.43 per cent to the variation in basic values. In the case of the Saharanpur respondents, the R^2 of 0.370 indicates that 37.0 per cent of the variation in basic values is explained, and the F value of 12.42 indicates a significant difference in the relative contribution of different components of knowledge. Among these elementary technical knowledge and skill, knowledge about agronomic practices, livestock practices, nutrition and health, and concern with philosophical and moral issues are significantly related with variation in basic values, and contribute 6.32 per cent, 11.17 per cent, 5.96 per cent, 10.70 per cent and 4.80 per cent, respectively, to its variation. In the case of the Trichur respondents, the R^2 of 0.061 indicates that only 6.1 per cent of the variation is explained by the nine components of cognitive orientation, and none of them is significantly related with variation in value orientation. The analysis on the whole indicates that it is knowledge about day-to-day activities (like crop and livestock farming, health matters and elementary technical knowledge) which significantly contributes to change in the basic values of the respondents.

Social Values

In Table 8.4, the regression coefficients, relative contribution of independent variables, R^2 and F values of the regression between the scores obtained on each of the nine dimensions of cognitive orientation, and the scores obtained on the twenty-two items of social values are given. At the aggregate level, the R^2 of 0.295 indicates that 29.5 per cent of the variation in values about social relations is explained. The F value of 27.43 is significant at the 1 per cent level, indicating that the relative contributions of different dimensions of the cognitive orientation vary. Among the nine components, knowledge about soil and plants, agronomic practices, livestock practices, nutrition and health, and knowledge about the

Table 8.4
Results of Multiple Regression Analysis between Values about Social Relations and Components of Cognitive Orientation

Cognitive Orientation	Azamgarh (N = 200)	Saharanpur (N = 200)	Trichur (N = 200)	Aggregate (N = 600)
1	2	3	4	5
1. Knowledge about soil and plants	−0.245	0.139	−0.051	0.271*
	(0.05)	(4.26)	(0.06)	(5.02)
2. Knowledge about natural phenomena	0.010	−0.333*	−0.076	−0.132*
	(0.05)	(3.66)	(0.29)	(4.21)
3. Elementary technical knowledge and skills	0.008	0.229	0.046	0.118
	(0.04)	(3.66)	(0.80)	(2.98)
4. Knowledge about agronomic practices	0.118	0.957†	0.180	0.502†
	(0.06)	(12.59)	(1.23)	(3.03)
5. Knowledge about livestock practices	0.119	0.179	0.406†	0.333†
	(1.71)	(2.61)	(6.26)	(6.70)
6. Knowledge about nutrition and health	0.345	0.717†	0.047	0.360†
	(3.04)	(10.27)	(0.33)	(5.43)
7. Knowledge about causation of diseases	0.025	0.343*	0.023	0.306†
	(0.21)	(4.04)	(0.40)	(10.70)
8. Knowledge about human fertility	0.088	−0.265	0.087	−0.056
	(1.40)	(0.45)	(1.48)	(1.05)
9. Concern with philosophical and moral issues	0.511*	0.089	−0.057	0.137
	(3.16)	(0.31)	(0.20)	(0.90)
	$R^2 = 0.097$	$R^2 = 0.345$	$R^2 = 0.102$	$R^2 = 0.295$
	$F = 2.28$*	$F = 11.14$†	$F = 2.39$*	$F = 27.43$†

Note: Figures in brackets indicate percentage of variation explained by an independent variable.
† = $P < 0.01$; * = $P < 0.05$.

causation of diseases are positively related with the value orientation. Knowledge about natural phenomena is negatively related with value orientation. The relative contribution of knowledge about the causation of diseases to changes in value orientation is

10.70 per cent, that of knowledge about livestock practices 6.70 per cent, knowledge about nutrition and health 5.43 per cent, knowledge about soil and plants 5.02 per cent, knowledge about natural phenomena 4.21 per cent, and knowledge about agronomic practices 3.03 per cent.

In the case of the Azamgarh respondents, the R^2 of 0.097 indicates that 9.7 per cent of the variation in social values is explained. The F value is significant at the 5 per cent level. Among the nine components of cognitive orientation, only concern with philosophical and moral issues is significantly related with variation in value orientation; it contributes 3.16 per cent to it. Knowledge about nutrition and health makes a contribution of 3.04 per cent to the variation in value orientation. In the case of the Saharanpur respondents, the R^2 of 0.345 indicates that 34.5 per cent of the variation in social values is explained. The F value of 11.14 is significant at the 1 per cent level, indicating significant difference in the relative contributions of the independent variables. The components of cognitive orientation significantly contributing to variation in values are knowledge about agronomic practices (12.59 per cent), and knowledge about nutrition and health (10.27 per cent). Knowledge about natural phenomena and human fertility are negatively related, and contribute 3.66 per cent and 0.45 per cent to variation in values. In the case of the Trichur respondents, the R^2 of 0.102 indicates that 10.2 per cent of the variation in value orientation is explained. Among the nine components of cognitive orientation, only knowledge about livestock practices is significantly related with the variation in values, contributing 6.26 per cent to its variation. Thus, the main components of knowledge which substantially contribute to change in social values are knowledge about nutrition and health, causation of diseases, and knowledge about crop and livestock farming activities.

Human Relations Values

In Table 8.5, the regression coefficients, relative contribution of independent variables, the R^2 and F values of regression between the scores obtained on the fifteen items of values about human relations and the scores obtained on the nine components of cognitive orientation are given. At the aggregate level, the R^2 of

Table 8.5
*Results of Multiple Regression Analysis between Values about
Human Relations and Components of Cognitive Orientation*

Cognitive Orientation	Azamgarh (N = 200)	Saharanpur (N = 200)	Trichur (N = 200)	Aggregate (N = 600)
1	*2*	*3*	*4*	*5*
1. Knowledge about soil and plants	−0.037 (0.43)	0.023 (0.53)	0.103 (1.05)	0.088 (2.34)
2. Knowledge about natural phenomena	0.052 (0.79)	−0.033 (1.08)	−0.005 (0.13)	0.029 (1.49)
3. Elementary technical knowledge and skills	0.051 (0.72)	0.006 (0.23)	0.044 (0.84)	0.063 (2.45)
4. Knowledge about agronomic practices	0.043 (0.02)	0.503† (11.61)	−0.148 (0.21)	0.209† (1.52)
5. Knowledge about livestock practices	0.210* (6.69)	0.249† (7.11)	0.030 (0.17)	0.247† (8.11)
6. Knowledge about nutrition and health	0.211 (3.57)	0.349† (11.13)	0.075 (0.56)	0.227† (5.33)
7. Knowledge about causation of diseases	0.062 (1.15)	0.128 (2.50)	0.071 (1.80)	0.020 (0.82)
8. Knowledge about human fertility	0.025 (0.54)	0.048 (1.08)	−0.065 (0.16)	−0.018 (0.50)
9. Concern with philosophical and moral issues	−0.120 (0.15)	0.120 (1.18)	−0.042 (0.07)	0.032 (0.25)
	$R^2 = 0.129$ $F = 3.11$†	$R^2 = 0.343$ $F = 11.02$†	$R^2 = 0.043$ $F = 0.94$	$R^2 = 0.213$ $F = 17.76$†

Note: Figures in brackets indicate percentage of variation explained by an independent variable.
† = $P < 0.01$; * = $P < 0.05$.

0.213 indicates that 21.3 per cent of the variation in values is explained by the nine components. The F value of 17.76, significant at the 1 per cent level, indicates significant difference in the relative contributions of the different components of knowledge.

Among these, knowledge about agronomic practices, livestock practices and nutrition and health are significantly related with variations in values, contributing 1.52 per cent, 8.11 per cent and 5.33 per cent, respectively, to the variation in values.

In the case of the Azamgarh respondents, the R^2 of 0.129 indicates that 12.9 per cent of the variation in value orientation is explained by the nine components of cognitive orientation. Among these, only knowledge about livestock practice is significantly related with variation in values, contributing 6.69 per cent to it. However, in the case of the Saharanpur respondents, the R^2 of 0.343 indicates that 34.3 per cent of the variation is explained, and the F value of 11.02 indicates that the relative contribution of each of these components differs significantly. Among the nine components, knowledge about agronomic practices, livestock practices and nutrition and health are significantly related with the variation in value orientation, contributing 11.61 per cent, 7.11 per cent and 11.13 per cent, respectively, to the variation in values. In the case of the Trichur respondents, only 4.3 per cent of the variation in value orientation is explained ($R^2 = 0.043$). The F value is not significant, indicating no significant variation in value orientation along with variation in knowledge. No component of cognitive orientation is significantly related with the variation in values.

Values about Agronomic Practices

In Table 8.6, the regression coefficients, R^2 and F values of regression between the scores on the four items of values about agronomic practices and the scores obtained on the nine components of cognitive orientation are given. At the aggregate level, the R^2 of 0.176 indicates that 17.6 per cent of the variation in value orientation about agronomic practices is explained by the nine components of cognitive orientation. The F value of 13.99, significant at the 1 per cent level, indicates significant variation in the relative contributions of the different components. Among the nine components, knowledge about soil and plants, elementary technical knowledge and skill, knowledge about agronomic practices and knowledge about livestock practices are positively related with variation in values, contributing 4.41 per cent, 4.79 per cent, 3.87 per cent, and 2.77 per cent to the variation, respectively. Knowledge about

Table 8.6
Results of Multiple Regression Analysis between Values about
Agronomic Practices and Components of Cognitive Orientation

Cognitive Orientation 1	Azamgarh (N = 200) 2	Saharanpur (N = 200) 3	Trichur (N = 200) 4	Aggregate (N = 600) 5
1. Knowledge about soil and plants	−0.072 (0.31)	0.109* (6.95)	0.053 (0.21)	0.075† (4.41)
2. Knowledge about natural phenomena	0.042 (0.67)	−0.081† (4.13)	−0.029 (0.81)	−0.034* (3.03)
3. Elementary technical knowledge and skills	0.042 (0.99)	0.082* (7.64)	0.025 (0.43)	0.053† (4.79)
4. Knowledge about agronomic practices	0.082 (0.94)	0.210† (12.00)	0.121* (2.07)	0.143† (3.87)
5. Knowledge about livestock practices	0.005 (0.06)	0.084* (5.14)	−0.024 (0.01)	0.047* (2.77)
6. Knowledge about nutrition and health	−0.024 (0.06)	0.129† (8.76)	−0.013 (0.00)	0.048 (2.13)
7. Knowledge about causation of diseases	−0.017 (0.07)	−0.017 (0.62)	0.011 (0.08)	0.025 (2.28)
8. Knowledge about human fertility	0.033 (1.35)	−0.026 (0.06)	−0.004 (0.02)	0.005 (0.30)
9. Concern with philosophical and moral issues	0.116 (1.83)	−0.067 (0.96)	−0.059 (0.92)	0.004 (0.07)
	$R^2 = 0.061$ $F = 1.38$	$R^2 = 0.342$ $F = 10.96†$	$R^2 = 0.045$ $F = 0.99$	$R^2 = 0.176$ $F = 13.99†$

Note: Figures in brackets indicate percentage of variation explained by an independent variable.
† = $P < 0.01$; * = $P < 0.05$.

natural phenomena is negatively related to variation in values,
contributing 3.03 per cent to the variation.

In the case of the Azamgarh respondents, only 6.1 per cent of
the variation in value orientation is explained, and none of the

components of cognitive orientation is significantly related with variation in values. The F value is not significant, implying that there is no significant variation in the relative contributions of different components of cognitive orientation. However, in the case of the Saharanpur respondents, the R^2 of 0.342 indicates that 34.2 per cent of the variation in values about agronomic practices is explained by the nine components of cognitive orientation. The F value of 10.96 indicates that the relative contributions of different components of knowledge differ significantly. Among them, knowledge about soil and plants, elementary technical knowledge and skill, knowledge about agronomic practices, livestock practices, and health and nutrition, make significant contributions of 6.95 per cent, 7.64 per cent, 12.00 per cent, 5.14 per cent and 8.76 per cent respectively, to the variation in value orientation. Knowledge about natural phenomena is negatively related, contributing 4.13 per cent to the variation in values. In the case of the Trichur respondents, the R^2 of 0.045 indicates that only 4.5 per cent of the variation in value orientation is explained by the nine components of cognitive orientation and, among these, only knowledge about agronomic practices makes a significant contribution of 2.07 per cent to the variation in values. These analyses indicate that there is considerable stability in values about agronomic practices. Whatever change has occurred in it may be attributed to variation in knowledge about agronomic practices, nutrition and health, and techniques and skill.

Values about Livestock Farming

In Table 8.7, the regression coefficients, relative contribution of independent variables, the R^2 and F values of regression between the scores obtained on the twelve items of values about livestock farming and the scores obtained on the nine components of cognitive orientation are given. At the aggregate level, the R^2 of 0.314 indicates that 31.4 per cent of the variation in values about livestock farming is explained by the nine components of cognitive orientation. The F value of 30.05 indicates that the relative contributions of different components of cognitive orientation to variation in value orientation differ at the 1 per cent level of significance. Among these, knowledge about agronomic practices, livestock

Table 8.7
*Results of Multiple Regression Analysis between Values about
Livestock Farming and Components of Cognitive Orientation*

Cognitive Orientation	Azamgarh (N = 200)	Saharanpur (N = 200)	Trichur (N = 200)	Aggregate (N = 600)
1	*2*	*3*	*4*	*5*
1. Knowledge about soil and plants	0.123 (1.92)	−0.201 (2.59)	0.028 (0.21)	0.045 (1.44)
2. Knowledge about natural phenomena	0.094 (2.00)	−0.019 (0.51)	0.027 (0.79)	0.047 (3.24)
3. Elementary technical knowledge and skills	0.011 (0.10)	0.079 (3.25)	0.004 (0.06)	0.042 (2.02)
4. Knowledge about agronomic practices	0.060 (0.11)	0.562† (14.31)	0.066 (0.27)	0.161* (0.92)
5. Knowledge about livestock practices	0.027 (0.35)	0.258† (7.94)	0.036 (0.23)	0.193† (6.98)
6. Knowledge about nutrition and health	0.060 (0.56)	0.244* (7.81)	0.044 (0.32)	0.109* (2.70)
7. Knowledge about causation of diseases	0.089 (2.04)	0.041 (0.59)	−0.004 (0.06)	0.169† (10.97)
8. Knowledge about human fertility	−0.059 (0.00)	0.062 (2.00)	−0.015 (0.07)	0.067* (2.96)
9. Concern with philosophical and moral issues	−0.028 (0.04)	0.136 (1.47)	−0.026 (0.04)	0.017 (0.20)
	$R^2 = 0.070$ $F = 1.60$	$R^2 = 0.343$ $F = 11.01†$	$R^2 = 0.017$ $F = 0.37$	$R^2 = 0.314$ $F = 30.05†$

Note: Figures in brackets indicate percentage of variation explained by an independent variable.
† = $P < 0.01$; * = $P < 0.05$.

practices, nutrition and health, causation of diseases, and control of human fertility are significantly related with the variation in value orientation, contributing 0.92 per cent, 6.98 per cent, 2.70 per cent, 10.97 per cent and 2.96 per cent, respectively, to the variation in value orientation.

In Azamgarh, the R^2 of 0.070 indicates that only 7.0 per cent of the variation is explained, and none of the components of cognitive orientation is significantly related with the variation in values. However, in the case of the Saharanpur respondents, the R^2 of 0.343 indicates that 34.3 per cent of the variation is explained, and the F value of 11.01 indicates that the variation in the relative contribution of different components to it varied significantly. Among the nine components of cognitive orientation, knowledge about agronomic practices, livestock practices and nutrition and health are significantly related with the variation in values, contributing 14.31 per cent, 7.94 per cent, and 7.81 per cent to the variation. In the case of the Trichur respondents, the R^2 of 0.017 indicates that only 1.7 per cent of the variation in values is explained, and none of the nine components of the cognitive orientation is significantly related with the variation. This means that, in Trichur, people with different levels of knowledge have similar type of values about livestock activities. But, in Saharanpur, those with more knowledge about agronomy, livestock farming and nutrition and health have more rational values about livestock activities.

Values about Nutrition and Health

In Table 8.8, the regression coefficients, relative contribution of independent variables, R^2 and F values of regression between the scores obtained on the nine items related to values about nutrition and health, and the scores obtained on the different components of cognitive orientation are given. At the aggregate level, the R^2 of 0.182 indicates that 18.2 per cent of the variation in values about nutrition and health is explained by the nine components of cognitive orientation, and the F value of 14.55, significant at the 1 per cent level, indicates significant variation in the relative contribution of each of these components. Among these, knowledge about natural phenomena, elementary technical knowledge and skill, knowledge about agronomic practices, nutrition and health, and concern with philosophical and moral issues, are significantly related with the variation in value orientation, and contribute, respectively, 5.19 per cent, 5.19 per cent, 2.91 per cent, 3.10 per cent, and 3.02 per cent, to the total variation.

In Azamgarh, the R^2 of 0.073 indicates that only 7.3 per cent of

Table 8.8
Results of Multiple Regression Analysis between Values about
Nutrition and Health and Components of Cognitive Orientation

Cognitive Orientation	Azamgarh (N = 200)	Saharanpur (N = 200)	Trichur (N = 200)	Aggregate (N = 600)
1	2	3	4	5
1. Knowledge about soil and plants	−0.076 (0.26)	−0.229* (3.19)	0.109 (1.57)	−0.028 (0.63)
2. Knowledge about natural phenomena	0.098 (0.77)˙	0.047 (1.37)	0.053 (2.59)	0.088* (5.19)
3. Elementary technical knowledge and skills	0.137* (1.32)	0.109 (4.19)	0.096 (2.67)	0.119† (5.19)
4. Knowledge about agronomic practices	0.267* (2.22)	0.636† (20.22)	0.338* (2.38)	0.274† (2.91)
5. Knowledge about livestock practices	0.008 (0.04)	0.103 (2.34)	−0.054 (0.09)	0.052 (1.21)
6. Knowledge about nutrition and health	0.080 (0.22)	0.175 (5.06)	0.182 (1.63)	0.147* (3.10)
7. Knowledge about causation of diseases	0.050 (0.00)	−0.005 (0.08)	−0.097 (0.97)	−0.013 (0.49)
8. Knowledge about human fertility	−0.114* (2.41)	−0.036 (0.70)	−0.075 (0.02)	−0.063 (1.33)
9. Concern with philosophical and moral issues	−0.046 (0.11)	0.416* (5.18)	0.270† (4.54)	0.231† (3.02)
	$R^2 = 0.073$ $F = 1.65$	$R^2 = 0.344$ $F = 11.07†$	$R^2 = 0.143$ $F = 3.53†$	$R^2 = 0.182$ $F = 14.55†$

Note: Figures in brackets indicate percentage of variation explained by an independent variable.
† = $P < 0.01$; * = $P < 0.05$.

the variation in values about nutrition and health is explained. Among the nine components, elementary technical knowledge and skill, and knowledge about agronomic practices are significantly related with value orientation, contributing 1.32 per cent and 2.22

per cent to its variation. Knowledge about fertility control is negatively related to it, contributing 2.41 per cent to the variation. In the case of the Saharanpur respondents, the R^2 of 0.344 indicates that 34.4 per cent of the variation in values about nutrition and health is explained. The F value of 11.07 indicates a significant difference in the relative contributions of different components. Among these, knowledge about agronomic practices and concern with philosophical and moral issues are significantly related with the variation in values, contributing 20.22 per cent and 5.18 per cent, respectively. Knowledge about soil and plants is negatively related with values about nutrition and health, and contributes 3.19 per cent to the variation in values. In the case of the Trichur respondents, the R^2 of 0.143 indicates that 14.3 per cent of the variation in value orientation is explained. The F value of 3.53 is significant at the 1 per cent level, indicating that the relative contributions of different components of cognitive orientation varied. Among them, knowledge about agronomic practices and concern with philosophical and moral issues are significantly related with the variation in values, contributing 2.38 per cent and 4.54 per cent to the variation in values. It is interesting to note that the respondents' scores on knowledge about nutrition and health have not made a positive contribution to modernisation of values about nutrition and health.

Values about Fertility Control

In Table 8.9, the coefficients, R^2 and F values of regression between respondents' scores on the thirteen items indicating their values about fertility control, and the nine components of cognitive orientation, are given. At the aggregate level, the R^2 of 0.202 indicates that 20.2 per cent of the variation in values about fertility control is explained by the nine components of cognitive orientation. The F value of 16.61, significant at the 1 per cent level, indicates a significant difference in the relative contributions of the different components. Among these, elementary technical knowledge and skill, knowledge about agronomic practices, and causation of diseases are significantly related with variation in values, contributing, respectively, 5.20 per cent, 1.74 per cent and 4.55 per cent, to the variation.

Table 8.9
Results of Multiple Regression Analysis between Values about
Fertility Control and Components of Cognitive Orientation

Cognitive Orientation	Azamgarh (N = 200)	Saharanpur (N = 200)	Trichur (N = 200)	Aggregate (N = 600)
1	2	3	4	5
1. Knowledge about soil and plants	−0.170 (0.05)	0.196 (4.25)	0.057 (0.33)	0.133 (2.99)
2. Knowledge about natural phenomena	0.356† (5.93)	−0.031 (0.83)	0.008 (0.16)	0.074 (3.50)
3. Elementary technical knowledge and skills	0.194 (2.08)	0.074 (2.04)	0.100 (2.48)	0.151† (5.20)
4. Knowledge about agronomic practices	0.042 (0.00)	0.592† (10.80)	0.139 (0.67)	0.277† (1.74)
5. Knowledge about livestock practices	−0.182 (1.19)	0.234 (4.75)	−0.074 (0.23)	0.065 (1.26)
6. Knowledge about nutrition and health	0.089 (0.38)	0.278 (6.10)	0.019 (0.12)	0.166 (2.75)
7. Knowledge about causation of diseases	0.149 (2.19)	0.060 (0.91)	0.012 (0.20)	0.166* (4.55)
8. Knowledge about human fertility	−0.064 (0.49)	−0.032 (0.28)	0.042 (0.48)	−0.055 (1.03)
9. Concern with philosophical and moral issues	−0.171 (0.08)	0.054 (0.35)	−0.212 (1.06)	−0.133 (0.75)
	$R^2 = 0.123$ $F = 2.96†$	$R^2 = 0.281$ $F = 8.24†$	$R^2 = 0.053$ $F = 1.17$	$R^2 = 0.202$ $F = 16.61†$

Note: Figures in brackets indicate percentage of variation explained by an independent variable.
† = $P < 0.01$; * = $P < 0.05$.

In the case of the Azamgarh respondents, the R^2 of 0.123 indicates that 12.3 per cent of the variation is explained, 'and among the nine components of cognitive orientation, only knowledge about natural phenomena is significantly related with the variation in values, making a contribution of 5.93 per cent to it. In the case of the Saharanpur respondents, the R^2 of 0.281 indicates that 28.1 per cent of the variation in value orientation is explained. The F value of 8.24 indicates that the relative contributions of the nine components to variation in values differ significantly. Among the nine components, only knowledge about agronomic practices is significantly related with the variation in values, making a contribution of 10.80 per cent. In the case of the Trichur respondents, only 5.3 per cent of the variation in value orientation is explained, and there is no significant variation in the relative contributions of different components of cognitive orientation, implying that respondents with different levels of knowledge have similar values about fertility control. It should be noticed that in none of the areas, is knowledge about fertility control practices significantly related with values about fertility control. Summarising the finding from the three areas, it can be said that it is knowledge about agronomic practices, nutrition and health, and livestock farming, which significantly influences the values about fertility control.

Commercial Values

In Table 8.10, the coefficients of regression between the scores obtained on the nine components of cognitive orientation and the scores obtained on the fourteen items of commercial values of the respondents, the R^2 and F values are given. At the aggregate level, the R^2 of 0.131 indicates that 13.1 per cent of the variation in commercial values is explained by the nine components of cognitive orientation. The F value of 9.88, significant at the 1 per cent level, indicates a significant difference in the relative contributions of different components to the cognitive orientation. Among the nine components, elementary technical knowledge and skill, knowledge about agronomic practices, knowledge about nutrition and health, and concern with philosophical and moral issues are positively related with variation in commercial values, and contribute 2.13 per cent, 5.24 per cent, 3.11 per cent and 1.20 per cent, respectively, to its variation. Knowledge related to human fertility is negatively related to variation in commercial values, and contributes 0.04 per cent to its variation.

In the case of the Azamgarh respondents, the R^2 of 0.033

Table 8.10
*Results of Multiple Regression Analysis between Commercial Values
and Components of Cognitive Orientation*

Cognitive Orientation	Azamgarh (N = 200)	Saharanpur (N = 200)	Trichur (N = 200)	Aggregate (N = 600)
1	*2*	*3*	*4*	*5*
1. Knowledge about soil and plants	0.044 (0.23)	−0.066 (0.85)	0.015 (0.11)	0.094 (1.32)
2. Knowledge about natural phenomena	−0.023 (0.06)	−0.158 (1.85)	0.020 (0.65)	−0.052 (1.06)
3. Elementary technical knowledge and skills	−0.075 (0.38)	0.252* (5.51)	0.003 (0.41)	0.102* (2.13)
4. Knowledge about agronomic practices	0.030 (0.04)	0.698† (12.98)	0.080 (0.01)	0.413† (5.24)
5. Knowledge about livestock practices	0.127 (1.92)	0.075 (0.90)	−0.212† (2.62)	0.083 (1.13)
6. Knowledge about nutrition and health	0.024 (0.04)	0.399† (7.09)	0.069 (0.62)	0.281† (3.11)
7. Knowledge about causation of diseases	0.026 (0.16)	0.203 (3.03)	−0.013 (0.19)	0.003 (0.06)
8. Knowledge about human fertility	−0.049 (0.02)	−0.236† (1.14)	0.027 (0.38)	−0.141† (0.04)
9. Concern with philosophical and moral issues	0.163 (0.70)	0.135 (0.64)	0.140 (2.46)	0.191* (1.20)
	$R^2 = 0.033$ $F = 0.72$	$R^2 = 0.286$ $F = 8.45†$	$R^2 = 0.071$ $F = 1.61$	$R^2 = 0.131$ $F = 9.88†$

Note: Figures in brackets indicate percentage of variation explained by an independent variable.
† = $P < 0.01$; * = $P < 0.05$.

indicates that only 3.3 per cent of the variation in commercial values is explained by the nine components of cognitive orientation. None of the components of cognitive orientation are significantly related with the variation in value orientation. However, in the case of the Saharanpur respondents, the R^2 of 0.286 indicates that 28.6 per cent of the variation in commercial values is explained by the nine components, and the relative contributions of different components to the variation in commercial values differ at the 1 per cent level of significance. Among these, elementary technical knowledge, knowledge about agronomic practices, and knowledge about nutrition and health are significantly related to variation in commercial values, respectively contributing 5.51 per cent, 12.98 per cent, and 7.09 per cent to the variation in commercial values. Knowledge about human fertility is negatively related to it, accounting for 1.14 per cent of the variation. In the case of the Trichur respondents, the R^2 of 0.071 indicates that 7.1 per cent of the variation in commercial values is explained by the nine components of cognitive orientation. The F value of 1.61 indicates that there is no significant difference in the relative contributions of different variables. Among them, only knowledge about livestock practices is significantly related with variation in values, making a contribution of 2.62 per cent. These analyses indicate that values about commercial activities are influenced to some extent through variation in knowledge, particularly by knowledge about agronomic practices, nutrition and health, and technical knowledge and skill.

Self-Assessment

In Table 8.11, the coefficients of regression between the self-assessment scores of the respondents, and the scores obtained by them on the nine components of cognitive orientation, and the R^2 and F values of the regressions are given. At the aggregate level, the R^2 of 0.102 indicates that 10.2 per cent of the variation in self-assessment is explained by the nine cognitive variables. The F value of 7.44 is significant at the 1 per cent level, indicating a significant difference in the relative contributions of different components. Among the nine components, elementary technical knowledge and skill, knowledge about nutrition and health, and knowledge about human fertility are significantly related with variation in self-assessment, contributing 4.22 per cent, 2.75 per cent and 4.21 per cent, respectively, to the variation in self-assessment.

In the case of the Azamgarh respondents, the R^2 value of 0.151

Table 8.11

*Results of Multiple Regression Analysis between Self-Assessment
and Components of Cognitive Orientation*

Cognitive Orientation 1	Azamgarh (N = 200) 2	Saharanpur (N = 200) 3	Trichur (N = 200) 4	Aggregate (N = 600) 5
1. Knowledge about soil and plants	−0.483* (0.92)	0.336 (1.49)	0.092 (0.49)	−0.219 (0.36)
2. Knowledge about natural phenomena	0.051 (0.03)	−0.377† (2.13)	−0.101 (1.92)	−0.067 (0.43)
3. Elementary technical knowledge and skills	0.075 (0.37)	−0.017 (0.27)	0.373† (9.55)	0.300† (4.22)
4. Knowledge about agronomic practices	−0.688* (3.76)	−0.354 (0.18)	0.796† (5.29)	0.012 (0.01)
5. Knowledge about livestock practices	0.245 (1.97)	−0.106 (0.63)	0.271 (2.20)	0.058 (0.37)
6. Knowledge about nutrition and health	0.388 (1.45)	0.378 (4.13)	0.320 (2.98)	0.390† (2.75)
7. Knowledge about causation of diseases	−0.287 (0.65)	0.433* (1.85)	0.111 (2.46)	−0.147 (0.60)
8. Knowledge about human fertility	0.130 (1.12)	0.648† (19.26)	0.295* (4.99)	0.258† (4.21)
9. Concern with philosophical and moral issues	1.061† (4.86)	0.604* (2.97)	−0.612† (1.07)	0.014 (0.03)
	$R^2 = 0.151$ $F = 3.76†$	$R^2 = 0.265$ $F = 7.61†$	$R^2 = 0.271$ $F = 7.85†$	$R^2 = 0.102$ $F = 7.44†$

Note: Figures in brackets indicate percentage of variation explained by an independent variable.
† = $P < 0.01$; * = $P < 0.05$.

indicates that 15.1 per cent of the variation in self-assessment has been explained, and the F value of 3.76 is significant at the 1 per cent level, indicating a significant difference in the relative contributions of different components of cognitive orientation. Among the nine variables, while respondents' knowledge about agronomic practices is negatively related with variation in values, concern with philosophical and moral issues is positively related with it. The former contributes 3.76 per cent and the latter 4.86 per cent to the variation in values. In the case of the Saharanpur respondents, the R^2 of 0.265 indicates that 26.5 per cent of the variation in self-assessment is explained. The F value of 7.61 is significant at the 1 per cent level, indicating significant variation in the relative contributions of different components of cognitive orientation. Among its nine components, knowledge about human fertility contributes 19.26 per cent to the variation. In the case of the Trichur respondents, 27.1 per cent of the variation is explained. The F value is also significant at the 1 per cent level. Among the nine components of cognitive orientation, elementary technical knowledge, knowledge about agronomic practices, human fertility control practices, and concern with philosophical and moral issues are related with variation in self-assessment, contributing 9.55 per cent, 5.29 per cent, 4.99 per cent, and 1.07 per cent, respectively, to the variation in self-assessment.

Aspiration for Economic Advancement

In Table 8.12, the coefficients of regression between the scores obtained on the nine components of cognitive orientation and the scores obtained on the five items measuring the level of aspiration of the respondents, and the R^2 and F values are given. At the aggregate level, the R^2 of 0.189 indicates that 18.9 per cent of the variation in the level of aspiration of the respondents for economic development is explained by the nine components of cognitive orientation. The F value of 15.30 indicates that the relative contributions of various components of cognitive orientation differ significantly. Among the nine components, elementary technical knowledge and skill, knowledge related to livestock practices, and knowledge about fertility control measures are positively related with the variation in aspiration, contributing 7.46 per cent, 6.20 per cent, and 6.22 per cent, respectively, to its variation. Knowledge about causation of diseases shows a negative relation, and contributes 1.87 per cent to the variation.

In the case of the Azamgarh respondents, the R^2 of 0.290

Table 8.12

Results of Multiple Regression Analysis between Aspiration for Economic Advancement and Components of Cognitive Orientation

Cognitive Orientation	Azamgarh (N = 200)	Saharanpur (N = 200)	Trichur (N = 200)	Aggregate (N = 600)
1	2	3	4	5
1. Knowledge about soil and plants	0.619*	−0.428*	−0.132	−0.212
	(7.43)	(1.26)	(1.16)	(1.10)
2. Knowledge about natural phenomena	−0.089	−0.107	0.001	0.029
	(0.80)	(0.37)	(0.06)	(0.41)
3. Elementary technical knowledge and skills	1.662†	0.064	0.246†	0.383†
	(10.61)	(1.01)	(11.06)	(7.46)
4. Knowledge about agronomic practices	−0.004	0.590†	0.347	0.222
	(0.07)	(2.29)	(3.18)	(0.34)
5. Knowledge about livestock practices	0.395*	0.368*	0.191	0.470†
	(6.37)	(3.67)	(2.63)	(6.20)
6. Knowledge about nutrition and health	−0.030	0.224*	0.228	0.085
	(0.16)	(2.28)	(3.51)	(0.61)
7. Knowledge about causation of diseases	0.171	−0.528*	0.077	−0.315†
	(3.15)	(2.38)	(3.08)	(1.87)
8. Knowledge about human fertility	0.113	0.669†	0.063	0.304†
	(1.79)	(21.33)	(1.47)	(6.22)
9. Concern with philosophical and moral issues	1.187	1.151†	0.027	0.164
	(0.59)	(6.94)	(0.14)	(0.65)
	R^2 = 0.290	R^2 = 0.408	R^2 = 0.237	R^2 = 0.189
	F = 8.64†	F = 14.55†	F = 6.55†	F = 15.30†

Note: Figures in brackets indicate percentage of variation explained by an independent variable.
† = $P < 0.01$; * = $P < 0.05$.

indicates that 29.0 per cent of the variation in the level of aspiration is explained by the nine components. The F value of 8.64, significant at the 1 per cent level, shows that the relative contributions of different components of the cognitive orientation to the level of aspiration of the respondents vary. Among the nine components, knowledge about soil and plants, technical knowledge and skill, and knowledge about livestock practices are significantly related with the variation in aspiration, respectively contributing 7.43 per cent, 10.61 per cent and 6.37 per cent to it. Knowledge about the causation of diseases contributes 3.15 per cent to its variation. In the case of the Saharanpur respondents, the R^2 of 0.408 indicates that 40.8 per cent of the variation in aspiration is explained by the nine components of cognitive orientation. The F value of 14.55 indicates that the relative contributions of different components of cognitive orientation vary. Among the nine components, knowledge about agronomic practices, livestock practices, nutrition and health, causation of diseases, human fertility control practices, and concern about philosophical and moral issues are positively related with the level of aspiration, and contribute 2.29 per cent, 3.67 per cent, 2.28 per cent, 2.38 per cent, 21.33 per cent and 6.94 per cent to the variation in the level of aspiration. Knowledge about soil and plants is negatively related with the level of aspiration and contributes 1.26 per cent to the variation. In the case of the Trichur respondents, the R^2 of 0.237 indicates that 23.7 per cent of the variation in the aspirational level is explained by the nine components of cognitive orientation. The F ratio of 6.55, significant at the 1 per cent level, indicates that the relative contribution of each component varied significantly. Among the nine components, elementary technical knowledge is significantly related with variation in aspiration, contributing 11.06 per cent to its variation.

The foregoing analyses indicate that the variation in value orientation explained by the nine components of cognitive orientation varies with the different dimensions of value orientation as well as with the areas. In Azamgarh, where a conservative cultural pattern prevails and where the level of knowledge is also very low, only a small proportion of the variation in value orientation is explained by variations in cognitive orientation. The picture from Trichur is similar, where both the cognitive and evaluative aspects of culture are very modern. The low variation in value orientation along with variation in knowledge in Trichur seems to be due to the widespread modernisation of values that has occurred in Trichur. In Saharanpur, where values are in transition, the percentage of variation in values explained by the variation in knowledge is very substantial, ranging from one-third to half of the variation.

Even though the relative contributions of different components of cognitive orientation to various dimensions of value orientation vary, the most important components of cognitive orientation which exercise significant influence on different dimensions of value orientation are knowledge about agronomic practices, livestock farming, nutrition and health, and elementary technical knowledge and skill. These cover the main activities on which the rural population are mostly engaged. The fact that knowledge about these activities greatly influences one's value orientation implies a strong relation between the pattern of knowledge and the pattern of value orientation prevailing in an area. Where knowledge about day-to-day activities is high, value orientation is more rational and modern; and inversely, where such knowledge is less, the value orientation is less rational and more traditional.

Inter-Correlation Among Components of Value Orientation

Values related to various aspects of life, or institutions, are not of equal significance; some values are more strongly believed than others. The basic or core values constitute the moral foundation of the society, by providing the frame of reference against which other values are evaluated. Through correlation analysis, an attempt has been made to understand the pattern of inter-relation among the different components of value orientation. As in the earlier cases, this analysis has been done for the aggregate sample of respondents, and for the sample of respondents from each of the areas. In Table 8.13, the coefficients of correlation among the ten components of value orientation are given for the aggregate sample. There is significant correlation among the values about social relations, basic values, commercial activities, fertility control, nutrition and health, livestock farming, and those about agronomic practices.

Among the ten components of value orientation, only self-assessment and aspiration for economic advancement are not related with other components of value orientation. Values about human relations are significantly related with basic values, values about commercial activities, fertility control, nutrition and health practices, livestock practices, agronomic practices, and social relations, at the 1 per cent level of significance. Basic values are similarly

Table 8.13

Correlation Matrix among the Various Components of Value Orientation (for the Aggregate Sample)

Dimensions of Value Orientation	Dimensions of Value Orientation									
	1	2	3	4	5	6	7	8	9	10
1. Social relations	1.000	—	—	—	—	—	—	—	—	—
2. Self-assessment	0.015	1.000	—	—	—	—	—	—	—	—
3. Aspiration for socio-economic advancement	0.102	0.295*	1.000	—	—	—	—	—	—	—
4. Basic values	0.354†	0.007	0.169	1.000	—	—	—	—	—	—
5. Commercial values	0.397†	0.017	0.170	0.390†	1.000	—	—	—	—	—
6. Control of fertility	0.448†	0.067	0.131	0.309†	0.283†	1.000	—	—	—	—
7. Nutrition and health	0.365†	−0.059	0.145	0.543†	0.437†	0.522†	1.000	—	—	—
8. Livestock practices	0.505†	0.067	0.165	0.367†	0.343†	0.532†	0.531†	1.000	—	—
9. Agronomic practices	0.409†	0.067	0.084	0.250†	0.266†	0.416†	0.342†	0.459†	1.000	—
10. Human relations	0.496†	0.056	0.180	0.370†	0.333†	0.478†	0.479†	0.523†	0.37	1.000

Note: † = P < 0.01; * = P < 0.05.

related with values about commercial activities, control of fertility, nutrition and health, livestock practices, agronomic practices, and human relations, apart from those about social relations. Values about commercial activities are related with values about fertility control, nutrition and health, livestock practices, agronomic practices, and values about human relations, besides values about social relations and basic values. Values about control of fertility are related with values about livestock practices, agronomic practices, human relations, social relations, basic values, commercial activities and fertility control. Values about livestock practices are related with values about agronomic practices, human relations, social relations, basic values, commercial values, fertility control, and values about nutrition and health practices. Values about agronomic practices are related with values about human relations, social relations, basic values, commercial activities, fertility control, nutrition and health, and livestock practices. And values about human relations are related with values about social relations, basic values, commercial activities, fertility control, nutrition and health, livestock practices, agronomic practices, and human relations. These findings indicate that there is a high degree of inter-relation among the various dimensions of value orientation. This means that rationalisation of values in one dimension of life spreads its influence to other dimensions.

In Table 8.14, the coefficients of correlation among the ten components of value orientation of the Azamgarh respondents are given. It is seen that the inter-relation among the different dimensions of value orientation is rather weak. Values about human relations are significantly related with values about social relations, control of fertility, nutrition and health, and livestock practices. The next highly correlated variable is values about nutrition and health, which is related with basic values and values about control of fertility. It is negatively related with values about socio-economic advancement. Values about livestock practices are related with values about control of fertility; values about agronomic practices with values about livestock practices; and values about commercial activities with values about economic advancement. Basic values are related with values about social relations.

In Table 8.15, the matrix of correlation among the different dimensions of value orientation of the Saharanpur respondents is given. There is a high degree of correlation among the various

Table 8.14

Correlation Matrix among the Various Components of Value Orientation (Azamgarh)

Dimensions of Value Orientation	Dimensions of Value Orientation									
	1	2	3	4	5	6	7	8	9	10
1. Social relations	1.000	—	—	—	—	—	—	—	—	—
2. Self-assessment	0.109	1.000	—	—	—	—	—	—	—	—
3. Aspiration for socio-economic advancement	0.109	0.099	1.000	—	—	—	—	—	—	—
4. Basic values	0.362†	-0.093	-0.070	1.000	—	—	—	—	—	—
5. Commercial values	0.020	-0.167	0.217*	0.046	1.000	—	—	—	—	—
6. Control of fertility	0.167	-0.027	-0.010	0.100	0.162	1.000	—	—	—	—
7. Nutrition and health	0.139	-0.201*	-0.093	0.314†	0.097	0.302†	1.000	—	—	—
8. Livestock practices	0.082	-0.048	0.095	0.070	-0.022	0.288†	0.142	1.000	—	—
9. Agronomic practices	0.110	0.083	0.031	0.126	-0.056	0.170	0.035	0.272†	1.000	—
10. Human relations	0.205*	0.062	0.104	0.123	0.046	0.197*	0.226*	0.346†	0.166	1.00

Note: † = P < 0.01; * = P < 0.05.

Table 8.15

Correlation Matrix among the Various Components of Value Orientation (Saharanpur)

Dimensions of Value Orientation	Dimensions of Value Orientation									
	1	2	3	4	5	6	7	8	9	10
1. Social relations	1.000	—	—	—	—	—	—	—	—	—
2. Self-assessment	0.060	1.000	—	—	—	—	—	—	—	—
3. Aspiration for socio-economic advancement	0.031	0.376†	1.000	—	—	—	—	—	—	—
4. Basic values	0.443†	0.259†	0.456†	1.000	—	—	—	—	—	—
5. Commercial values	0.593†	0.110	0.149	0.627†	1.000	—	—	—	—	—
6. Control of fertility	0.464†	0.202*	0.137	0.423†	0.476†	1.000	—	—	—	—
7. Nutrition and health	0.419†	0.184	0.285†	0.631†	0.585†	0.612†	1.000	—	—	—
8. Livestock practices	0.454†	0.312†	0.291†	0.580†	0.545†	0.548†	0.654†	1.000	—	—
9. Agronomic practices	0.452†	0.120	0.125	0.373†	0.429†	0.471†	0.488†	0.471†	1.000	—
10. Human relations	0.599†	0.159	0.156	0.474†	0.467†	0.503†	0.536†	0.548†	0.502*	1.000

Note: † = $P < 0.01$; * = $P < 0.05$.

dimensions of value orientation, except those of self-assessment and aspiration for socio-economic advancement. The values of many of these correlations are very high, indicating the strong inter-relation among those dimensions. Values about social relations are significantly related with basic values, values about commercial activities, fertility control, nutrition and health, livestock practices, agronomic practices, and human relations. Self-assessment is related with values about economic advancement, basic values, control of fertility, and livestock practices. Aspiration for economic advancement is significantly related with basic values, values about nutrition and health, and values about livestock practices. Basic values of the respondents are highly correlated with all the other dimensions of values. Values about commercial activities are highly correlated with all other components of values, except self-assessment, and values about economic advancement. Values about fertility control are significantly related with all other components of value orientation, except aspiration for economic advancement, and values about agronomic practices. Values about nutrition and health are related with all other dimensions of values, except self-assessment and agronomic practices. Values about livestock practices are significantly related with all the other dimensions of value orientation. Values about agronomic practices are related with all the other components of value orientation, except self-assessment and aspiration for socio-economic advancement. Values about human relations are also related with all the other components, except self-assessment and aspiration for economic advancement. It is thus seen that there is a high degree of inter-relation among the different dimensions of value orientation of the Saharanpur respondents.

In Table 8.16, the coefficients of correlation among the ten dimensions of value orientation of the Trichur respondents are given. Though these correlations are not as strong as in the case of the Saharanpur respondents, the pattern is broadly similar. Values about social relations are significantly related with self-assessment, aspiration for socio-economic advancement, and values about human relations. Respondents' self-assessment is significantly related with their aspiration for socio-economic advancement, and values about nutrition and health; but is negatively related with basic values. Aspiration for socio-economic advancement is not significantly related with any of the other components of value

Table 8.16

Correlation Matrix among the Various Components of Value Orientation (Trichur)

Dimensions of Value Orientation	Dimensions of Value Orientation									
	1	2	3	4	5	6	7	8	9	10
1. Social relations	1.000	—	—	—	—	—	—	—	—	—
2. Self-assessment	0.199*	1.000	—	—	—	—	—	—	—	—
3. Aspiration for socio-economic advancement	0.358†	0.432†	1.000	—	—	—	—	—	—	—
4. Basic values	−0.048	−0.234*	−0.053	1.000	—	—	—	—	—	—
5. Commercial values	−0.105	−0.064	−0.112	0.118	1.000	—	—	—	—	—
6. Control of fertility	0.140	−0.005	0.119	0.247*	0.114	1.000	—	—	—	—
7. Nutrition and health	0.056	0.304†	−0.061	0.610†	0.352†	0.294†	1.000	—	—	—
8. Livestock practices	0.136	−0.039	−0.109	0.224*	0.250*	0.249*	0.361†	1.000	—	—
9. Agronomic practices	0.149	0.049	0.054	0.016	0.107	0.302†	0.111	0.213*	1.000	—
10. Human relations	0.235*	−0.131	0.019	0.417†	0.126	0.453†	0.371†	0.395†	0.157	1.000

Note: † = $P < 0.01$; * = $P < 0.05$.

orientation. The basic values of the respondents is positively related with values about fertility control, nutrition and health, livestock practices, and values about human relations. The values of the respondents about commercial activities are significantly related with values about nutrition and health, and livestock practices. Values about fertility control are related with basic values, values about nutrition and health, livestock practices, agronomic practices, and human relations. Values about nutrition and health are related with self-assessment, basic values, values about commercial activities, fertility control, nutrition and health, and human relations. Values about livestock practices are related with basic values, values about commercial activities, fertility control, nutrition and health, agronomic practices, and social relations. Thus, in the case of the Trichur respondents also, a high degree of correlation is seen among the various dimensions of value orientation.

The high degree of correlation among the different dimensions of value orientation indicates that a certain degree of coherence exists among the various dimensions of value orientation. As a result, the pattern of values orientation in one dimension is influenced by, and influences, the pattern of value orientation in other dimensions. This gives the value orientation pattern of an area its distinctive feature.

Principal Components of Value Orientation

The high degree of correlation among the ten components of value orientation implies their relevance for understanding the value orientation of the respondents. Through principal component analyses, those components of value were identified which are the principal components of value orientation. The results of the analyses, for the first rotation, are given in Table 8.17. Items with loadings of 0.35 and above are treated as significant. The variance explained is 39.88 per cent in the case of the aggregate sample; 21.56 per cent in the case of the Azamgarh respondents; 47.79 per cent in Saharanpur; and 27.41 per cent in the case of the Trichur respondents. Variables with loadings of 0.35 and above are significant, and the components of value orientation with loadings above this level are values about livestock farming, values about nutrition and health, values about human relations, social values,

Table 8.17
*Principal Components of Value Orientation, with the Values
of the First Component of the Ten Variables*

Components of Values	Azamgarh	Saharanpur	Trichur	Aggregate
1. Social values	0.3622*	0.3183	−0.0540	0.3611*
2. Self-assessment	−0.1148	0.1470	0.1961	0.0412
3. Aspiration for socio-economic advancement	0.0469	0.1671	0.0714	0.1380
4. Basic values	0.3623*	0.3556*	−0.4148*	0.3157
5. Commercial values	0.0187	0.3503*	−0.2529	0.3005
6. Values about control of fertility	0.3977*	0.3349	−0.3556*	0.3603*
7. Values about nutrition and health	0.4003*	0.3749*	−0.4741	0.3784*
8. Values about livestock farming	0.3937*	0.3695*	0.3742	0.3874*
9. Values about agronomic practices	0.2878	0.3049	−0.1931	0.3169
10. Values about human relations	0.4069*	0.3432	−0.4348*	0.3680*
Percentage of variance by first component	21.56	47.79	27.41	39.88

Note: * = loadings of 0.35 and above are significant.

and values about the control of fertility in the case of the aggregate sample. In the case of the Azamgarh respondents, the significant components are values about human relations, nutrition and health, control of fertility, livestock farming, basic values, and social values. In the case of the Saharanpur respondents, they are values about nutrition and health, livestock farming, basic values, and commercial values; and in Trichur, values about nutrition and health, human relations, basic values, livestock farming, and control of fertility.

Among the various components, three components are common in all the three areas. They are the basic values, values about nutrition and health, and values about livestock farming, implying that they constitute the core of the value system. It was seen earlier that the mean scores obtained by the respondents on these three components varied significantly. The lowest scores on all of them were obtained by respondents from the less developed area of Azamgarh, while the highest score was obtained by the respondents from the developed area of Trichur. Thus, there is a coherence between the level of socio-economic development of an area and the pattern of culture prevailing in that area.

Summary

In this chapter, the relation between the cognitive and evaluative dimensions of culture was examined. The analysis was done jointly for the aggregate sample of respondents, and separately for the respondents from each area. The analysis was also done jointly for the different dimensions of value orientation, and separately for each dimension. Through regression analysis, the relative contributions of different components of cognitive orientation to variation in value orientation were estimated. This showed that cognitive orientation made a significant contribution to variation in value orientation. Though there was some divergence in their details, the central tendency revealed through the analyses was that knowledge about agronomic practices, livestock practices, nutrition and health, and elementary techniques and skill uniformly contributed to change in value orientation. These are the activities on which villagers spend most of their time, and the increase in knowledge about these activities contributes to the rationalisation and secularisation of values. Inversely, ignorance is an important basis of superstition and tranditionalism.

Through principal component analyses, the most crucial components of values were isolated. The values common to all the areas were those about basic values, values about nutrition and health, and values about livestock farming.

A high degree of correlation was observed between the different dimensions of value orientation. This implies a certain coherence among the different dimensions of value orientation, with change in one dimension affecting other dimensions. It is generally believed that culture, particularly value orientation, is stable. However, it is seen that though values have a great degree of stability and autonomy, they are prone to change. While the direct influence of socio-economic forces in creating changes in values is weak, knowledge is an important force in the rationalisation and modernisation of values. Inversely, lack of knowledge is an important reason for the sustenance of many traditional customs and values.

9

Summary of Findings, Conclusions and Implications

The objective of this study is to understand the pattern of culture in areas varying in levels of socio-economic development. Culture is defined as patterns, explicit and implicit, of and for behaviour, acquired and transmitted by symbols. Its essence is traditionally derived ideas and their attached values. While a cultural system is a product of action, it is a conditioning element for further action. Though external to an individual, through the process of socialisation culture becomes internalised, becoming a part of the individual's personality, making it a source of motivation. The main components of culture are knowledge, philosophical ideas, ideology and religious beliefs. Even though theoretically it is possible to have such fine distinctions, at the empirical level, such classifications are rather difficult. Therefore, in this study, a broader division of culture into cognitive ideas, or knowledge, and evaluative ideas or values, was adopted.

Development is multidimensional, and apart from increase in wealth, it involves factors such as control of diseases, improvement in health, reduction in fertility, and improvement in environmental and personal hygiene. These require knowledge to pursue appropriate kinds of action, and values emphasising their pursuit. For example, if fertility reduction is to be achieved, there should be both the knowledge to practise fertility control measures and values emphasising small families.

A variety of factors (like natural resources, capital, technology, knowledge, values and social organisation) contribute to the development of an area. Culture, comprising knowledge and values, constitutes one of these factors, rather than its sole determinant. Economic development can be pushed through the use of other means also, but its pace can be quickened if the cultural component is harnessed, and integrated with the overall development process. To cite a concrete example, while executing an irrigation project, attention is generally given only to its technological and to some extent its agronomic aspects, rather than creating appropriate values and knowledge among the people using the irrigation facility. If this aspect is also covered, the utilisation of irrigation facilities, the productivity of the farms, and the earnings of the farmers and, therefore, the overall effectiveness of an irrigation project, is likely to be greater. Culture being a component of the socio-economic system, its pattern has to be in coherence with other aspects of the economy and society. This is the central hypothesis of this study and, based on this, it was postulated that the pattern of culture in areas with different levels of socio-economic development would vary. It is likely to be characterised by greater knowledge and more rational values in developed areas, and less knowledge and less rational values in less developed areas.

The study to understand cultural patterns was conducted in Phulpur block, Azamgarh district, eastern Uttar Pradesh; Rampur block, Saharanpur district, western Uttar Pradesh; and Anthikadu block, Trichur district, Kerala. From each of these blocks, a sample of 200 respondents was selected through a two-stage random sampling procedure. The respondents were interviewed through a questionnaire between October 1984 and January 1985, in order to obtain the requisite information. An understanding of the characteristics of the respondents would give an idea of the level of development of the three areas.

Socio-Economic Background

More than three-fourths of the respondents in all the areas were Hindus, and most of them belonged to the middle level castes. Among the household members above six years, illiterates formed more than two-thirds in Azamgarh, 45 per cent in Saharanpur, and 6 per cent in Trichur. The average landholdings of the respondents in the three areas were 195 cents in Azamgarh, 246 cents in Saharanpur, and 49 cents in Trichur. Those without any land formed 16 per cent of the respondents in Azamgarh, 55 per cent in Saharanpur and 2 per cent in Trichur. The average value of livestock, the other important asset, was Rs 2,781, Rs 5,329 and Rs 783 respectively, in the three areas.

The average size of the household was 8.0 in Azamgarh, 7.2 in Saharanpur and 5.2 in Trichur. Household members below eleven years constituted 34 per cent of the household members in Azamgarh and Saharanpur and 16 per cent in Trichur, indicating the drastic decline in fertility in Trichur.

Among the respondents, 63 per cent from Azamgarh, 48 per cent from Saharanpur and 12 per cent from Trichur were cultivators, and 13 per cent, 24 per cent and 25 per cent worked as agricultural labourers. The average monthly earning per household was Rs 551 in Azamgarh, Rs 1,182 in Saharanpur, and Rs 626 in Trichur; the per capita monthly earnings were Rs 69, Rs 164 and Rs 120. The main source of income in Azamgarh and Saharanpur was agriculture, while in Trichur it was employment.

The life-style in the three areas varied. The modal group in Azamgarh lived in *kacha* houses, cooked food in earthen vessels, used cow-dung fuel, and were not accustomed to using latrines and bathrooms. Compared to this, in Saharanpur, the modal group lived in *pucca* houses, cooked food in stainless steel vessels, used fuel from agricultural wastes, and were not accustomed to the use of latrines and bathrooms. In Trichur, the modal group lived in *kacha* houses, cooked food in aluminium vessels, used fuel from agricultural wastes, and also used latrines and bathrooms.

Paddy and wheat are the main crops cultivated in Azamgarh and Saharanpur, respectively, during the kharif and rabi seasons. In Trichur, paddy and coconut are the main crops. Since paddy is a common crop in all the areas, its yield may be taken to compare agricultural development in the three areas. It is 9.4 quintals per acre in Azamgarh, 18.7 quintals in Saharanpur and 17.1 quintals in Trichur. In Azamgarh, most of the agricultural products are domestically consumed, but in Saharanpur and Trichur a major part of it is marketed.

Characteristics of Culture

The main hypothesis of the study is that the pattern of knowledge and values in areas with different levels of development varies. To understand the pattern of knowledge prevailing in the three areas, respondents' knowledge on the following nine aspects were examined: natural phenomena, characteristics of soil and plants, agronomic practices, livestock practices, causation of diseases, nutrition and health, fertility control, technical knowledge and skill, and concern with philosophical and moral issues. A number of questions were put to the respondents in order to understand their level of knowledge on each of these components, and the responses to each component was scored by giving a value 0 for a response indicating lack of knowledge on an item, and a score of 1 for a response indicating knowledge about an item. Through this process, nine indices of cognitive orientation were developed. The mean scores obtained by the respondents from the three areas on each of these indices was computed, and through them the level of knowledge about different aspects of day-to-day life prevailing among the respondents from the three areas was compared. Through F and HSD statistics, the significance of the variation in the mean scores from the three areas were examined. The results of these analyses are given in Table 9.1. The average scores obtained by the respondents on the nine indices indicate that there is significant difference in the level of knowledge of the respondents from the three areas in each component of knowledge examined. The level of knowledge on each component is the lowest in Azamgarh, the least developed area, higher in Saharanpur and the highest in Trichur, indicating that there is a coherence between the level of development of an area and the pattern of knowledge prevailing in that area.

Some of the main findings about the characteristics of knowldege may be highlighted. Knowledge about natural phenomena is particularly low among the Azamgarh and Saharanpur respondents, with only a few of them knowing about phenomena like the rotation of the earth, occurrence of the wind and rain, while knowledge about such matters is higher in Trichur. Knowledge about the characteristics of soil and plants is also lower in Azamgarh, higher in Saharanpur and the highest in Trichur. Similarly, there is a sharp difference among the respondents from the three areas about the causation of diseases. The causation of many of the ordinary diseases are unknown to the Azamgarh respondents. Similarly, knowledge about nutrition and health, fertility control practices, and technical knowledge and skill is also low among the

Table 9.1

*Mean Scores Obtained by Respondents on Various Indices
of Knowledge and the Results of Statistical Tests*

Indices of Knowledge	No. of Items	Azamgarh	Saharanpur	Trichur	Results of F Test
1. Natural phenomena	13	0.92	3.04	6.36	†
2. Characteristics of soil and plants	9	3.62	4.24	5.97	†
3. Agronomic practices	5	2.99	2.78	2.57	†
4. Livestock practices	12	7.31	8.15	9.59	†
5. Causation of diseases	17	4.10	4.39	9.21	†
6. Nutrition and health	8	3.45	3.28	4.44	†
7. Fertility control	12	5.52	5.37	8.50	†
8. Technical knowledge and skill	15	5.67	6.71	8.70	|
9. Concern with philosophical and moral issues	3	0.65	0.60	1.38	†

Note: † = P < 0.01.

Azamgarh respondents. Knowledge about all these matters is more widespread in Saharanpur and Trichur.

In order to understand the pattern of value orientation of the respondents, the types of values held by the respondents in respect of the following aspects were studied: basic values, social values, values about human relations, agronomic practices, livestock farming, nutrition and health, fertility control, commercial activities, self-assessment, and aspiration for socio-economic advancement. The type of values held by the respondents was understood by seeking their responses on value-loaded statements. Utilising these responses, 10 indices of value orientation were developed by scoring the responses on each dimension of value orientation. While scoring the responses, a value of 0 was given for a response indicating subscription to a traditional/conservative value, and a value of 1 was given to a response indicating belief in a modern value. The mean scores obtained by the respondents on the ten dimensions of value orientation and the results of the statistical tests examining the significance of their variations are given in Table 9.2. It is seen that the value orientation of the respondents from the three areas differed significantly on each of the dimensions

Table 9.2

Mean Scores Obtained by Respondents on Various Indices
of Value Orientation and the Results of Statistical Tests

Indices of Value Orientation	No. of Items/ Scores	Azamgarh	Saharanpur	Trichur	Results of F Test
1. Basic values	11	4.93	5.01	5.78	†
2. Social values	22	11.38	12.60	16.02	†
3. Human relations	15	8.03	9.66	10.03	†
4. Agronomic practices	4	2.36	2.53	3.10	†
5. Livestock farming	12	6.30	7.37	9.88	†
6. Nutrition and health	9	3.95	5.01	5.71	†
7. Fertility control	13	6.60	8.21	9.51	†
8. Commercial values	14	6.96	7.85	7.60	†
9. Self-assessment	30	8.97	10.18	8.76	†
10. Aspiration for socio-economic advancement	25	13.38	17.50	15.09	†

Note: † = $P < 0.01$.

examined. On each dimension, the lowest scores were obtained by the Azamgarh respondents, indicating that the most conservative/ traditional values prevailed among them. On the other hand, the scores obtained by the Saharanpur respondents were higher, and the highest scores were obtained by the Trichur respondents, indicating the prevalence of more modern values in developed areas. Thus, a certain amount of coherence is seen between the cognitive and evaluative dimensions of culture and the level of development of an area.

Some characteristics of value orientation may be indicated. It was found that in all the areas, there was great emphasis on the salvation of the soul, conformity to traditional practices, and fatalism. Among occupational values, occupations like pisciculture and hogging were mostly evaluated on non-economic criteria, like purity and pollution, and honorific and non-honorific, subordinating economic rationality to ritual evaluation. The pattern of values about dietary and health matters was similar. The ritual qualities of food were strongly cherished, subordinating its nutritive qualities. There was widespread fatalism about health and related matters, with the majority of the respondents believing that one was likely to die at the predestined time and of a predestined cause. Values about fertility control were quite popular, and there was a general acceptance of the desirability of small families. Values about commercial activities were less congenial for the development of commerce. There was emphasis on self-reliance of the household and the village, and a distrust of traders and strangers. Thus, the respondents had predominantly traditional value orientation. While respondents from Azamgarh held the most traditional values, some amount of modernisation was found in Saharanpur, and still greater change in Trichur.

Correlates of Empirical Knowledge

Analyses were done through multiple regression analyses to locate factors contributing to variation in knowledge. These analyses were done for the aggregate sample and the sample from each area, and also for each of the components of cognitive orientation as also by aggregating the nine components of knowledge, and developing an aggregate index of knowledge. The scores obtained by the respondents were the dependent variables, and the contribution of the following eight independent variables to the variation of the dependent variables was examined—respondents' education, their fathers' education, membership in associations, exposure to mass media, spatial mobility, types of tools used, value of inputs used and per capita monthly household income. In Table 9.3, the percentage of variance in knowledge explained by the eight independent variables (socio-economic characteristics) is given. At the aggregate level, for the whole sample (N = 600), and the aggregate index of cognitive orientation, the regression analyses explained 54.4 per cent of the variation in the level of knowledge by the eight independent variables. Exposure to mass media, education of self and fathers' education were found to be the most important variables contributing, respectively, 29.29 per cent, 10.72 per cent and 5.84 per cent to the variation in the level of knowledge. The percentage of variation explained was 29.1 in Azamgarh, 48.3 in Saharanpur and 41.5 in Trichur. The main variables associated with the change in knowledge were exposure to mass media in Azamgarh and Saharanpur, and education in Trichur.

The proportion of variation in the individual components of knowledge explained by the eight socio-economic characteristics

Table 9.3

Percentage of Variation in Different Components
of Knowledge Explained by Independent Variables

Component of Knowledge	Azamgarh	Saharanpur	Trichur	Aggregate
1. Knowledge about natural phenomena	20.0	35.1	24.5	38.4
2. Knowledge about soil and plants	13.7	26.7	16.5	31.6
3. Knowledge about agronomic practices	7.4	9.6	19.5	1.6
4. Knowledge of elementary techniques and skills	33.0	32.5	39.0	42.6
5. Knowledge about livestock practices	19.3	2.6	15.8	31.7
6. Knowledge about nutrition and health	10.3	3.2	18.9	23.2
7. Knowledge about causation of diseases	12.3	20.1	23.9	34.4
8. Knowledge about human fertility	13.5	18.5	23.5	24.2
9. Concern with philosophical and moral issues	13.6	29.7	8.9	16.6
10. Aggregate index of knowledge	29.1	48.3	41.5	54.4

varied. The most important factor contributing to the variation differed with the area and the component of knowledge. Since the variation in nine components of knowledge was examined in relation to four groups (three area samples and the total sample), there were 36 regression tests to identify the relative contribution of various factors to variation in knowledge. Among these 36 tests, as many as 23 indicated mass media as being the most important variable contributing to variation in knowledge. The importance of mass media as a source of change was found in all the areas. Education of the respondents was found to be the most important source of change in five'cases, and its influence was the most pronounced in Trichur, where the level of education among the respondents was quite high. No other independent variable was found to be consistently related with variation in the different dimensions of knowledge.

Correlates of Values

In Table 9.4, the percentage of variance in different dimensions of value orientation explained by the eight independent variables is given. By and large, only a small percentage of the variation has been explained in all the areas, indicating the relative stability of value orientation despite changes in socio-economic characteristics. The total variance explained is the highest (31.4 per cent) in the case of the overall index of value orientation of the whole group, and the most important factors causing this change was exposure to mass media (19.97 per cent), and education (4.49 per cent), again indicating the crucial role of these two factors in bringing about cultural change.

The main factor causing change in the case of each component of value orientation in the three areas and at the aggregate level was identified through regression analysis. Out of the 40 such

Table 9.4

*Percentage of Variation in Different Dimensions
of Values Explained by Independent Variables*

Dimensions of Value	Azamgarh	Saharanpur	Trichur	Aggregate.
1. Basic values	13.1	16.0	7.0	7.6
2. Social values	6.7	13.2	5.0	20.6
3. Values about human relations	8.0	9.1	7.1	13.2
4. Values about agronomic practices	11.5	9.8	4.6	12.3
5. Values about livestock farming	3.7	11.5	6.3	23.6
6. Values about nutrition and health	3.7	10.3	7.7	12.0
7. Values about fertility control	6.8	16.0	4.8	17.3
8. Values about commercial activities	9.5	10.9	11.6	3.7
9. Self-assessment	10.3	20.5	18.3	20.6
10. Aspiration for socio-economic advancement	31.2	15.0	19.0	17.0
11. Overall index of value orientation	20.3	21.3	21.9	31.4

analyses, exposure to mass media was the most important factor bringing about change in 22 cases, indicating the predominant roll of mass media as a contributor to change. The influence of mass media in this respect was found in all the areas and at the aggregate level. Education was the most important factor bringing about change in six cases, and its influence in this respect was predominant in Trichur. Spatial mobility and membership in associations were found to be important sources of change in Saharanpur. Thus, by and large, it is exposure to mass media and education which are the predominant factors bringing about change in the value orientation of the respondents.

Inter-Relation between Knowledge and Values

Since knowledge and values are two dimensions of culture, a certain degree of relation between the two was envisaged. Correlation tests showed a high degree of relation between the various dimensions of knowledge and values. These relations were found to be quite strong in all the three areas, and at the aggregate level. The aggregate index of cognitive orientation and different indices of cognitive orientation were highly related with the overall index of value orientation, and various individual indices of value orientation. These relations indicate that knowledge is a powerful cause of change in value orientation.

Regression analyses were done to estimate the relative contribution of different components of knowledge to variation in values. The regression at the aggregate level between the overall index of values and the aggregate index of knowledge indicated that 42.0 per cent of the variation in values was due to variation in knowledge. The important components of knowledge contributing to this variation were knowledge about elementary techniques and skill (12.64 per cent), livestock practices (10.19 per cent), and knowledge about nutrition and health (9.29 per cent). A similar pattern was seen at the regional levels also. Further regressions were carried out between the various dimensions of values and the different components of knowledge. These analyses also showed that variation in each dimension of value was caused through change in knowledge. Among the 40 such analyses, knowledge about agronomic practices was found to be the first component of knowledge contributing to change in values in 12 cases, followed by elementary technical knowledge and skill contributing the maximum change in seven cases, and knowledge about livestock practices contributing the maximum change in six cases. All components of knowledge contributed to change in some dimension of value orientation, indicating that there is a certain degree of diffuse relation among the different components of knowledge and dimensions of value orientation.

It was also seen that at the aggregate level there was a high degree of inter-relation among the various dimensions of values. Among the ten dimensions of value orientation, only self-assessment and values about economic advancement are not significantly related with other dimensions of values. However, in the case of the Azamgarh respondents, the main association was between values about nutrition and health and basic values and control of fertility, between values about livestock practices and control of fertility, and between values about livestock practices and agronomic practices and human relations. In the case of the Saharanpur respondents, all dimensions of values, except self-assessment, were strongly inter-related. Among them basic values, values about livestock practices, fertility control, and human relations were strongly related with other dimensions. And in Trichur basic values, values about nutrition and health and human relations were strongly related with other dimensions. The predominance of basic values, values about nutrition and health, and value about livestock practices in the value orientation pattern of the respondents was also found through principal component analyses, indicating that they constituted the core of the value orientation of the respondents.

Conclusions and Implications

The foregoing findings indicate significant variation in the pattern of culture in the three areas varying in their level of development. Such a variation in culture was found to be significantly related with variation in the socio-personal characteristics of the population, particularly their exposure to mass media and level of education. This is in confirmity with the findings of scholars like Daniel Lerner and Alex Inkles, who identified education and mass media exposure as the main sources of modernisation. The strong inter-relation between variation in knowledge and variation in values suggests that expansion in knowledge caused through education, and exposure to mass media are the principal cause of the variation in value orientation in the three areas. Though exposure to mass media was the main source of change in knowledge and values in Azamgarh and Sharanpur, it was education which was the principal source of this change in Trichur. The reason why education was not the most important source of cultural change in Azamgarh and Saharanpur may be due to the underdevelopment of education in these two areas, with illiterates constituting more than two-thirds of the population in Azamgarh, and 45 per cent of the population in Saharanpur. Though education can spread as an independent factor, economic development is an important cause of the spread of education, bringing changes in the cultural framework of the society.

The close inter-relation between cognitive and evaluative orientations, between different components of knowledge and various dimensions of value orientation, and the inter-relation among various dimensions of value orientation reflect the integrated nature of culture, with change in any one sector having repercussions on other sectors. It was seen that though change in the peripheral layers of culture (like the pattern of production and to some extent in the pattern of knowledge) is fast, change in value orientation, constituting the core of the culture, is a slow process. But change occurs even in this core aspect. This implies that as no man needs to remain traditional in outlook because he was born in a society, no society also needs to remain eternally traditional, limiting the capacity of its members to fully exploit the potential available in their environment to lead a richer life.

The finding that the pattern of culture in an area is in congruence with the level of socio-economic development of that area implies that culture is the component of the production system, influencing the pattern of production as well as being influenced by the pattern of production. Though the most important factor bringing about change in it was found to be exposure to mass media, in the area where education has spread, it has become the most important source, significantly contributing to expansion in knowledge and the rationalisation of values. This finding is in conformity with the writings of several scholars emphasising that education plays a crucial role in economic development.

Even though non-cultural factors themselves can push through socio-economic development, their effectiveness will be greater and the process of development will be smoother and quicker if the cultural dimension of development is also built into the development programme. The case of irrigation was mentioned earlier. The role of culture is important for other developmental programmes also. For example, a scheme for rural drinking water supply can be more effective if information about diseases caused through contaminated water, and the causes of water contamination are disseminated in the community along with the construction of the water supply project. Similarly, schemes for constructing latrines in rural areas can be more effective if information about the health hazards posed by defecating in the open is spread in the community.

The cultural dimension of development programmes is not generally appreciated, and little efforts are made to build this component as well into development programmes. If this is done, the effectiveness of the developmental programme will be greater.

References

Alexander, K.C. 1980. 'Economic Development and Social Change', *Behavioural Sciences and Rural Development*, Vol. 3, No. 2: 91–132.

―――――. 1982. 'Agricultural Development and Social Transformation: A Study in Ganganagar, Rajasthan', *Journal of Rural Development*, Vol. 1, No. 1: 1–71.

―――――. 1985. 'A Study of Agricultural Development and Social Transformation', *Journal of Rural Development*, Vol. 4, No. 5: 565–611.

Chandra, Bipin. 1965. 'Reinterpretation of Nineteenth Century Indian Economic History', *The Indian Economic and Social History Journal*, Vol. 5.

Dube, S.C. 1963. 'Cultural Problems in the Economic Development of India', in R.N. Bellah, ed, *Religion and Progress in Modern India*, New York: Free Press.

―――――. 1976. 'Social and Cultural Factors in Development', Yogesh Atal and Ralph Pieris, eds, *Asian Development: A Symposium*. New Delhi: Abhinav.

Harbison, Frederick and **Charles Myres.** 1964. *Education, Manpower and Economic Growth*. McGraw Hill, New York.

Inkles, Alex and **David H. Smith.** 1974. *Becoming Modern: Individual Change in Six Developing Countries*. London: Heinemann.

Kapp, William. 1963. *Hindu Culture, Economic Development and Economic Planning in India*. Bombay: Asia Publishing House.

Kluckhohn, R.K. and **Strodtbeck, F.L.** 1961. *Variations in Value Orientation*. New York: Row Petersons and Company.

Kroeber, A.L. 1948. *Anthropology*. New York: Harcourt, Brace and Company.

―――――― and **Clyde Kluckhohn.** 1952. 'Culture: A Critical Review of Concepts and Definitions', *Harvard University Peabody Museum of American Archeology and Ethnology Papers*, Vol. 47, No. 1, Cambridge, Mass.

Leibenstein, Harvey. 1957. *Economic Backwardness and Economic Growth: Studies in the Theory of Economic Development*, New York: Wiley.

―――――. 1978. *General X-Efficiency Theory of Economic Development*. New York: Oxford University Press.

Lerner, Daniel. 1964. *The Passing of Traditional Society: Modernization in the Middle East*. New York: Free Press.

Lewis, Arthur. 1957. *Theory of Economic Growth*. London: Allen and Unwin.

C.P. Loomis, and **Z.K. Loomis.** 1964. *Socio-Economic and Religious Factors in India*. New Delhi: Affiliated East-West Press.

Mandalbaum, David G. 1974. *Human Fertility in India.* Berkeley: University of California Press.

McClelland, David C. 1961. *The Achieving Society.* Princeton: Van Nostrand Co.

Mishra, Vikas. 1962. *Hinduism and Economic Growth.* London: Oxford University Press.

Narayanaswami, Indira. 1981. *The Religion, Family and Economic Activity of the Nattukottai Chettiars: Re-examination of the Weberian Thesis on Religion and Economy.* Pune: Gokhale Institute of Politics and Economics.

Nevaskar, Balvant. 1971. *Capitalists Without Capitalism.* Connecticut: Greenwood Publishing Corporation.

Parsons, Talcott. 1951. *The Social System.* London: Tavistock Publications.

————— *et. al.* 1953. *Working Papers in the Theory of Action.* New York: Free Press.

————— and **Edward Shills,** eds, 1959. *Towards a General Theory of Action.* Cambridge: Harvard University Press.

—————. 1963. 'The Motivation of Economic Activities', in *Essays in Sociological Theory.* Glencoe: The Free Press.

Rao, M.S.A. 1969. 'Religion and Economic Development', *Sociological Bulletin.* Vol. 18, No. 1, March.

Schultz, Theodore. 1963. *Economic Value of Education.* New York: Columbia University Press.

Singer, Milton. 1956. 'Cultural Values in India's Economic Development' in *The Annals of the American Academy of Political and Social Sciences,* May.

Srinivas, M.N. 1958. 'A Note on Mr Goheen's Note', *Economic Development and Cultural Change,* Vol. 7, No. 1.

Tilman, R.G. 1963. 'The Influence of Caste on Indian Economic Development' in R. Braibanti and J.J. Spengler, eds, *Administration and Economic Development in India.* Durham: Duke University Press.

Timberg, Thomas A. 1978. *The Marwaris.* New Delhi; Vikas Publishing House.

Tylor, Edward B. 1871. *Primitive Culture.* Mass: Gloucester.

Von Oppen, M., Parthasarathy Rao and **K.V. Subba Rao.** 1985. 'Impact of Market Access on Agricultural Productivity in India', *Economic and Social Development: Some Issues.* Hyderabad: NIRD.

Weber, Max. 1952. *Protestant Ethnic and the Spirit of Capitalism.* London: George Allen and Unwin Ltd.

—————. 1958. *The Religion of India: The Sociology of Hinduism and Buddhism,* trans. by Hans H. Gerth and Don Martindale. Glencoe: The Free Press.